FROM LOKSHEN TO LO MEIN

The Jewish Love Affair with Chinese Food

The Kosher Chinese Cookbook

Donald Siegel

gefen גפן
publishing house בית הוצאה לאור
JERUSALEM ● NEW YORK Est. 1981

Typesetting by S. Kim Glassman
Cover Photographs by Tony Golden
Cover Design by Sherri Taylor
Illustrations by Esther Siegel
Chinese Calligraphy by Li Jin

3 5 7 9 8 6 4

Gefen Publishing House
6 Hatzvi Street, Jerusalem 94386, Israel
972-2-538-0247
orders@gefenpublishing.com

Gefen Books
600 Broadway, Lynbrook, NY 11563, USA
1-800-477-5257
orders@gefenpublishing.com

www. israelbooks.com

Printed in Israel

Send for our free catalogue

ISBN: 965-229-357-1

FIRST, A QUIP

Chinese history dates back about 5000 years and Jewish culture dates back about 6000 years. The question is, how could the Jews survive for the first thousand years without Chinese food?

CONTENTS

Acknowledgements 11

Memories and Foreword 13

An Introduction to Chinese Cooking and Cuisine 15

    The Many Kinds of Chinese Cuisine 15

    The Evolution of Chinese Cooking 17

The Jewish Experience in China...19

The American-Jewish Chinese Connection.............................21

For the Non-Jewish Reader: What is Kosher? 25

    Kashrut Laws and Chinese Food 26

    Kosher Chinese Products 27

CHINESE COOKING TECHNIQUES

    General Preparation 32

    Chopping and Slicing 32

    Wok Cooking..33

    Stir-Frying..34

        A Basic Stir-Fry Dish 35

5

All Purpose Stir-Fry Sauce 36

Steaming.. 36

The Drop Dead Tip for Making a Chinese Dinner 37

The Chinese Kitchen Cabinet 37

THE KOSHER CHINESE RECIPES

Where are the Recipes From?.. 39

On Seasoning... 40

On Meat Substitutions 40

On Stir-Frying 40

On Deep-Fat Frying 41

On Thickening, Marinating and Tenderizing 41

On Rice Cooking 42

Preparing a Full Meal 42

Chef's Hints 42

Other Chinese Kosher Cookbooks... 43

SOUPS

Chicken Stock... 47

Vegetable Stock 48

Egg Drop Soup 49

Soup Wontons 50

Corn Soup 52

Hot Sour Soup 53

Chrysanthemum Hot Pot 54

West Lake Soup 56

Banquet Soup.. 57

APPETIZERS (DIM SUM)

Chicken Wings.. 60

    Wings Karper 61

    Soy Wings 62

    Peanut Wings... 63

Dumplings.. 65

    Dumpling Skins 66

Making Dumplings 67

    Basic Dumpling Sauce 70

    Hunan-Style Dumplings 71

    Vegetarian Dumplings 72

    Spicy Dumplings with Sesame Sauce 73

    Seafood Dumplings 75

    Soup-Filled Juicy Dumplings 76

Spring Rolls and Egg Rolls 79

    Vegetarian Spring Roll 81

    Meat and Noodle Spring Roll 82

Buns 85

    Basic Dumpling Dough 86

    Steamed Buns (The Traditional Way)........................ 87

    Baked Buns 88

    Pan-Fried Pot Sticker Buns... 89

    Chicken-Filled Buns 90

    Mushroom Cashew Buns 91

    Barbequed Meat Buns 92

    Curry Buns 93

ASSORTED DIM SUM

Onion Cakes 96

P.F. Chang's Lettuce Wraps 97

Paper-Wrapped Chicken....................................99

Tea Eggs.. 101

Fish Toast 102

Sweet and Sour Daikon Radish........................ 103

Hot Spicy Cabbage.. 104

Candied Pecans or Walnuts.............................. 105

NOODLES AND RICE

Ants Climbing a Tree 109

Lo Mein with Peanut Sauce 111

Chow Fun.. 113

Chow Mein 115

Noodles in Brown Sauce 117

Szechwan Noodles 118

Fried Rice.. 120

VEGETARIAN

Broccoli Salad.. 125

Cold Sweet and Sour Chinese Cabbage 126

Vegetable Mu Shu.. 127

Mandarin Pancakes 128

Szechwan Spicy Eggplant................................. 129

Stir-Fried Spinach or Other Greens................... 131

Tofu and Mushrooms in Vinegar Sauce............. 132

Mapo Tofu.. 133

Deep-Fried Chinese Greens 135

Double Cooked String Beans 136

FISH

Steamed Fish with Ginger and Scallions 139

Salt and Pepper Fish Strips 141

Stir Fried Fish Strips with Asparagus 142

Asian Fish in Packets 143

Braised Hot and Sour Fish 144

Red Cooked Whole Fish 146

Sweet and Sour Fried Fish 148

CHICKEN, DUCK AND OTHER FOWL

Steamed Chicken with Soy Scallion Sauce 153

Red Cooked Chicken 154

Kung Pao Chicken 156

General Tso's Chicken 158

Chinese Style Oven-Fried Chicken 160

Uncle Tai's Diced Chicken with Walnuts 162

Rock Sugar-Ginger Chicken with Tofu and Chestnuts 164

Moo Goo Gai Pan 166

Braised Chicken with Ginger 168

Chinese Roast Chicken 169

Roast Barbequed Turkey Served in Steamed Yeast Buns 170

Steamed Yeast Buns 171

Egg Foo Yung 172

Lemon Chicken 173

Roast Duck in a Bag 175

Tea-Smoked Duck Breast 177

Pan Roasted Duck 179

BEEF

Beef with Ginger and Garlic 183

Beef with Onions 184

Beef with Broccoli 185

Braised Curried Beef and Potatoes 186

Lamb with Leeks 187

Beef or Lamb with Scallions 188

Red Cooked Beef 190

Spicy Szechwan Beef 191

DESSERTS

Almond Cookies 195

Sweet Walnut or Peanut Soup 196

Sweet Buns with Bean Paste 197

Almond Float 198

Chinese Pancakes with Apricot Filling and Peanuts 199

Banana and Ginger Wontons with Chocolate Sauce 201

Crystallized Ginger 203

Banana-Pecan Spring Rolls with Caramel-Rum Sauce 204

Five Spice Roasted Pears 206

Deep-Fried Bananas with Syrup and Toasted Sesame Seeds 207

Selected References 209

Index of Ingredients and General Items 211

Index of Recipes 221

ACKNOWLEDGEMENTS

Thanks to Marjory Baruch, Wu-Teh Hsiang and Rabbi Daniel Jezer for kindly reviewing this book for both Jewish and, in the Baruch and Hsiang case, Chinese content. I am especially grateful to my wife Bette for her professional editing and her Asian "fusion" dessert recipes. I thank Hannah Siegel for the preliminary editing of the manuscript and Esther Siegel for the illustrations.

I offer special thanks to Master Chef Simon Teng, owner of the China Road Restaurant in Mattydale, New York, for his advice and encouragement. His own exquisite cuisine remains a benchmark for my own cooking.

I am grateful to my many culinary "patrons" at Congregation Beth Sholom-Chevra Shas, DeWitt, New York. These wonderful friends celebrate my Chinese cooking and prompted me to write this book.

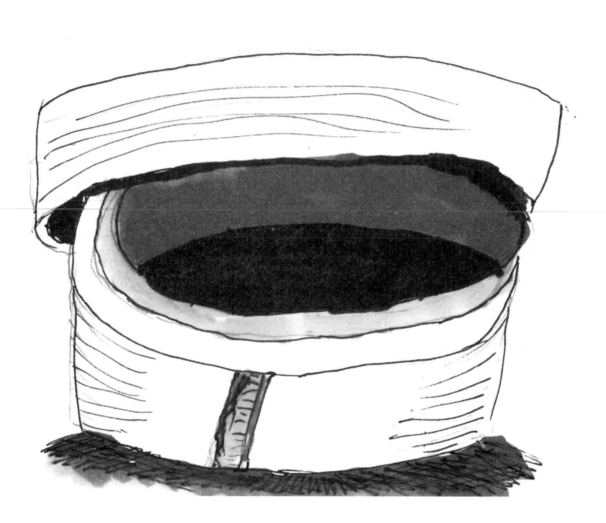

MEMORIES AND FOREWORD

Over the past decade, I have had the pleasure of catering 10-course Chinese banquets as fundraisers for Congregation Beth Sholom-Chevra Shas, a Conservative synagogue in DeWitt, New York. All catering must be kosher, and yet I am still able to prepare classic Chinese dishes such as Roast Duck, Whole Gingerroot and Scallion Steamed Fish and Assorted Dim Sum (special Chinese appetizers). Many congregants have asked me to make my recipes available, and this book is, in part, my response to their requests.

This book also includes some reflections on the "connection" between Chinese cooking and Jews. I grew up in Saratoga Springs, New York, and one of my earliest childhood memories in the 1950s is being taken by my parents to eat at Lum Fung's Cantonese Chinese Restaurant. Invariably, my father ordered egg rolls for the table, then egg drop soup with wontons, followed by Moo Goo Gai Pan (chicken with mushrooms) or sweet and sour chicken. My mother would order Shrimp in Lobster Sauce.

I wondered why we ritually observant Jews could eat egg rolls and wontons that had bits of non-descript chopped meat in them, as well as, in my mother's case, outright *treif* (non-kosher) shrimp. As I grew older, I realized that traditional ritual observance for Jews is mostly personal preference; even ultra-observant Hassidic sects fight over whose version of kashrut is most ritually pure!

In time, Chinese food made it to our home in the form of canned chop gooey (suey) made by La Choy or Chung King companies. Mom warmed up these cans of sauced meat and vegetables and slathered them onto cardboard-dry chow mein noodles. My grandmother, "Bubbe" Bessie Siegel, warmed to the task and began to make her own chow mein noodles, preparing Russian kreplach (dumpling) dough into tasty fried noodles which were a marked improvement over the commercial products.

Bubbe then began making her own version of chow mein itself: chopped celery, assorted meats, water chestnuts, scallions, a bit of sherry, organ meats and La Choy kosher soy sauce, thickened with cornstarch. Bubbe's attempt at making chow mein was far closer to the real thing than I knew at the time. To this day, I remember the flavors of her homemade chow mein, the actual recipe for which was never written down, given Bubbe's ad-libbing style of cooking. Mom also realized that Chung King products could be improved upon, and began to experiment with "Jewish-Chinese" recipes.

The "connection" between Chinese food and Jews truly came to my attention a few years ago when a new Chinese restaurant, China Road, opened near our hometown, Syracuse. The owner, Simon Teng, is an internationally known Master Chef from New York City.

An Asian student of mine at Syracuse University first told me about Simon's restaurant and so I tried it out. The food was fabulous, and I later submitted a short review of China Road's food to the local newspaper. The review was published, and Simon told me that his business exploded – as much with Jews as Asians. When I attended synagogue, friends complained that they now had to wait in line at China Road, whereas before, it was one of their little culinary "treasures."

Along with my favorite Chinese kosher recipes, I include some comments on the connection between Jews and Chinese culture; where to get kosher Chinese ingredients; a few jokes about Jews and Chinese food; a short section on what "kosher" means for those unfamiliar with Jewish dietary laws; and digressions on Chinese cooking techniques and products.

Some classic Jewish foods are analogous to Chinese versions – hence my title, *From Lokshen to Lo Mein*. *Lokshen* are Jewish noodles used in many recipes, an analogue to lo mein noodles used in Chinese cooking.

AN INTRODUCTION TO CHINESE COOKING AND CUISINE

THE MANY KINDS OF CHINESE CUISINE

The Chinese probably enjoy eating even more than the French. Cooking is a Chinese art; some of the very best Chinese restaurants in America are modest establishments in the back streets and other Chinese enclaves of "Chinatowns," far away from the tourist sections.

Many experts roughly classify Chinese food into four major culinary regions: the northern plains, including Beijing; the fertile east, drained by the Yangtze River; the south; and the western Szechwan and Hunan Provinces.

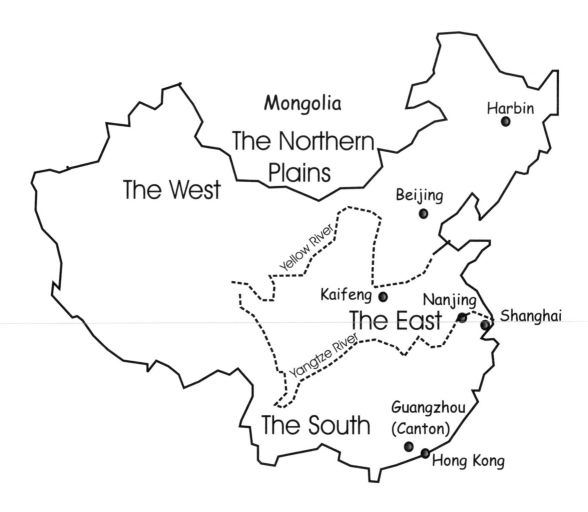

The Chinese immigrants that came to America in the 1800s were mostly from the Cantonese (modern Guangzhou) region in southern China. Their cooking emphasized freshness: seafood, rice and vegetables prepared with subtlety. Traditional Cantonese women in Hong Kong make daily trips to markets to buy the freshest possible produce. Steaming and stir-frying are the preferred Cantonese cooking styles. A classic Cantonese dish is a simple steamed whole fish with ginger sauce.

In contrast to Cantonese cooking, people living in the mountainous and isolated hot and cold regions of western Szechwan and Hunan prepared salted, pickled and spicy foods redolent with hot pepper, ginger, garlic, chili peppers, onions and brown peppercorns. A famous Szechwan recipe is tea-smoked duck, first marinated in orange peel, sherry, cinnamon and other spices, steamed and finally smoked with wood chips, sugar and tea leaves. Yummy.

People living in hot, humid eastern China cook a wide array of rice and seafood dishes sweeter than in other regions. Braised, stewed and deep-fried foods are popular. "Red-cooking," where meat is simmered in a soy and licorice-flavored sauce, originated in eastern China.

Finally, the nomads of northern China and desert Mongolia prepare lamb, wheat-based steamed breads and noodles. Chinese fondues, called "hot pots," originated in northern China.

Just as Paris is the center of French food, Beijing is where Chinese imperial "haute" cuisine was born in the kitchens of the emperors. Imperial banquets could include 365 dishes, one for each day of the year. Many Americans are familiar with Roast Beijing Duck, which is one of the banquet dishes from the imperial tradition.

In China, as in the United States, people from different culinary regions often view the cuisine of other regions with, if not disdain, a certain lack of appreciation. My wife Bette and I have a Chinese friend, Al Young, from Guangdong (Canton). When Bette was pregnant with our son, Micah, Al prepared for her Chicken Braised with Ginger. He said this dish would relieve her morning sickness and lead to a healthy baby. When I commented on how much we enjoyed Szechwan cuisine, he scoffed and said, "No subtlety, no subtlety!"

THE EVOLUTION OF CHINESE COOKING

Chopsticks were invented around 5000 years ago as a substitute for knives. Chinese cooking evolved to its great sophistication during the Chow Dynasty from 1050–221 B.C.E. when the great Chinese philosopher and teacher, Confucius, established both culinary standards and table etiquette. Food is cut into bite-sized pieces during preparation in the kitchen rather than at the table, and cutting food at the table is considered a sign of aggression and boorish behavior.

Confucius taught that flavors must be blended and balanced with harmony, including: color, taste, aroma, presentation and texture. Food attributes are treated almost like primary colors: "*La*" means hot and spicy; "*Tian*" means sweet; "*Suan*" means sour; "*Xian*" means salty; and "*Ku*" means bitter. "*Ma*" is a spicy flavor unique to Szechwan cooking. "*Xian*," or salty, is an essential attribute of much Chinese cooking.

Chinese dishes are designed as mixtures of these essential food attributes. For example, "salty and spicy," "*xian-la,*" is typical of Szechwan cooking; whereas "*tian-suan,*" or sweet-sour, is typical of Cantonese and eastern cooking styles. The balancing of flavor attributes is essential in good Chinese cooking.

The Chinese also classify foods as "hot" or "cold," referring to the "temperament" of the food rather than its serving temperature. For example, fatty foods prepared with hot spices are "hot," whereas poached vegetables and fruit are "cold."

The philosophy of Taoism, which also evolved when Confucius lived, emphasized food that was healthy. Taoist cooks discovered that improper cooking destroys nutritional values of vegetables, and that garlic and ginger have medicinal values, a fact which is recognized even today.

THE JEWISH EXPERIENCE IN CHINA

The Jewish Diaspora included China as well as other far-flung migrations from Europe to India and Africa. Jewish merchants entered China during the Middle Ages along the famous Silk Road passing through Afghanistan. A viable Jewish community existed in China from the eighth century to almost the present day.

In the thirteenth century Marco Polo wrote that he met Jews in China and reported that the famous emperor, Kublai Khan, celebrated Jewish festivals. As elsewhere, Judaic traditions that evolved in China became different from those in Europe and the Middle East. Chinese Jewish lineage became patriarchal rather than matriarchal.

The first synagogue in China was built in the city of Kaifeng in 1163. Kaifeng Jews were so accepted that a Ming dynastic emperor gave them official surnames: Ai, Lao, Jin, Li, Shi, Zhang and Zhao. Jesuit missionaries, as late as the eighteenth century, described Jewish daily life and religious practices in Kaifeng.

The Kaifeng and other Jewish communities of China are now assimilated, and their Jewish-Chinese religious artifacts were sold off during the nineteenth century. Much later, Jewish refugees from Europe fled to Shanghai, China, as World War II began in the late 1930s. There, however, the Jewish population remained separate from the greater Chinese community around it, and so the Jewish-Chinese connection was less intense than in Kaifeng.

THE AMERICAN-JEWISH CHINESE CONNECTION

Why do American Jews so love Chinese food? Two sociologists, D. Tuchman and H. Levine, argue that the Jewish love for Chinese food began in New York City during the early 1900s. Then, Jewish immigrants lived in the Lower East Side of Manhattan next to Chinatown. Chinese and Eastern European Jewish foods have some common ingredients, such as chicken, fish, cabbage, celery, garlic and onions. Perhaps because Jews were already familiar with these foods, they developed a taste for Chinese cooking. Chinese cooks seldom use milk products; so Jews eating in Chinatown knew there would be little chance that rabbinic prohibitions against mixing dairy and meat products would be broken in a Chinese restaurant.

Chinese food may also have been "exotic" to Jewish immigrants; eating in Chinese restaurants was one way to acculturate within the larger American society. Certainly, Chinese food was exotic to my family when I grew up.

Finally, some American Jews consider Chinese food as "safe *treif*," i.e., if you can't identify the ingredients, then it is ok to eat it. "*Treif*" is a Yiddish word meaning food that is ritually prohibited, not allowed according to the laws of kashrut (hence the expression of "not being kosher"). The notion of safe *treif* is a very American lay interpretation of kashrut. Philip Roth even mentions it in his famous book *Portnoy's Complaint*. The concept, of course, completely contradicts numerous rabbinic directives that a Jew cannot eat *anything* with which he or she is unfamiliar!

In any case, the linkage between Chinese food and Jews is strong. One of my colleagues at Syracuse University, a Chinese mathematician, Wu-Teh Hsiang, converted to Judaism before marrying another mathematician, Marjory Baruch, who is Jewish. At a family party, Marjory's Aunt Gert, a wonderful comedian, asked Wu-Teh if he liked Chinese food. Wu-Teh replied, "Of course, I'm Jewish!"

Although Jews eat "Chinese" all times of the year, they really flock to Chinese restaurants immediately before and after Passover and on Christian religious holidays when other restaurants are closed. *The New York Times* even had a full article on this Jewish holiday tradition, highlighting New York City's Shun Lee Dynasty, a famous Chinatown restaurant. There, it was reported that fully 70% of the patrons are Jewish; so the owner feels that, "Giving them a home away from home on Christmas Day makes perfect sense."

The tradition of Jews eating Chinese food on Christmas has been immortalized in a famous parody of "The Night Before Christmas," excerpted below:

'Twas the Night Before Jewish Christmas (*Anon*)

My girlfriend and I had nothing to do.
The Gentiles were home, hanging stockings with care,
Secure in their knowledge St. Nick would be there.
But for us, once the Hanukkah candles burned down,
There was nothing but boredom all over the town.

Outside the window sat two feet of snow;
With the wind-chill, they said it was fifteen below.
And while all I could do was sit there and brood,
My girl saved the night and called out, "CHINESE FOOD!"

In search of a restaurant: "Which one? Let's decide!"
We chose "Hunan Chozer" and ventured inside.

Around us sat other Jews, their platters piled high
With the finest of foods their money could buy.

Before us sat dim sum, spare ribs and egg rolls,
And four different soups, in four great, huge bowls.
The courses kept coming from spicy to mild,
And higher and higher toward the ceiling were piled.

The MSG spun round and round in my head,
As we tripped and we laughed and gaily we said,
While we carried our leftovers home through the night;
"Good Yom Tov to all – and to all a Good Night!"

Most Americans, Jews included, are familiar with Chinese-American style Chinese food. Chinese-American cooking evolved to appeal to broad American tastes, much as "Tex-Mex" cooking of the southwestern states appeals to Americans. The sweeter and thicker sauces of Chinese American cooking really exploded on the American scene in the 1950s when two Minnesotans, Jeno Paulucci and his Jewish friend David Persha, introduced canned Chun King brand kosher Chinese chow mein to supermarkets. These two businessmen realized that American soldiers returning from the Pacific theater of WW II had developed a taste for Asian food. Chun King products began with Chicken Chow Mein, a concoction of blended Italian and Chinese ingredients served on dry chow mein noodles with soy sauce and hot Chinese mustard on the side. Chun King dominated the canned Chinese-American food market for decades.

In contrast to Chinese-American food, authentic Chinese cuisine varies from chef to chef. A Chinese-American Kung Pao Chicken in Des Moines will taste about the same as one in Syracuse. However, eating an authentic Whole Fish Steamed with Ginger and Scallions or Chow Fun (a noodle dish) will be different everywhere you go. Such is great cooking.

FOR THE NON-JEWISH READER: WHAT IS KOSHER?

"Kosher" or kashrut, refers to the dietary laws adhered to by ritually observant Jews. Non-kosher food is called *treif*. The origin of the Jewish (and to some extent, Moslem) dietary laws is the Torah, the "five books of Moses." Since the Torah evolved thousands of years ago, Jews have adhered to kashrut laws differently, depending upon cultural circumstances and evolving rabbinic interpretations.

Very briefly, the dietary laws of kashrut itemized in the Torah are:

- Mammals and permitted fowl must be ritually slaughtered.
- Only mammals that chew their cud and have completely cloven hooves can be eaten. Jews cannot eat pigs or horses.
- Only seafood with scales and fins can be eaten. This rule eliminates mollusks (clams, oysters) and crustaceans (shrimp and lobster).
- The young of allowed mammals should not be cooked in their mother's milk.

Rabbis over the millennia have expanded in their interpretations (*halacha*) of kashrut laws to include many other prohibitions, some of which are:

- Red meat and fowl must be soaked in salt to remove blood.
- Milk products of any kind cannot be mixed with red meat or fowl.
- "Prepared" foods must be cooked under the supervision of a ritually acceptable rabbi.

Jews in the Reform and Reconstructionist branches sometimes adhere to fewer halachic kashrut rules than Jews associated with Conservative and Orthodox affiliations. Jews descended from European communities (Ashkenazi) even have some different kashrut traditions from those in the Middle East (Sephardic). Prepared foods in the United States that have been rabbinically ruled as kosher have a "*hekshur*," a kosher symbol, on the label, such as an "OU" or "Star-K."

Non-Jews and Jews alike ask, "Why are there kashrut laws?" No one really knows for sure. One common explanation is that kashrut originated from health concerns; pigs can give humans trichinosis and shellfish can cause botulism.

Another explanation is that the farmers and Bedouins of the ancient Middle East despised pigs, which, being smart, refuse to be herded. Early Jews, who lived in the interior regions of the Middle East, were perhaps unfamiliar with shellfish popular on the Mediterranean coast.

Finally, eating is a fundamental part of living. Some rabbis think that the laws of kashrut were devised to constantly remind Jews of their unique place in history and relationship with their God. Keeping kashrut in this context involves daily personal discipline.

KASHRUT LAWS AND CHINESE FOOD

Pork and shellfish figure prominently in Chinese cooking. However, Jews who keep kosher don't have to deprive themselves from eating excellent Chinese food. Even vegetarians need not worry – Chinese Buddhists developed a highly-sophisticated vegetarian cuisine with mock meat of every kind. My own Chinese banquets and dinners feature many vegetarian dishes. In major North American cities, including Toronto, Chicago, Philadelphia,

New York, Los Angeles and San Francisco, there are Chinese restaurants certified kosher by Orthodox rabbis.

Many Jews have personal stories about kashrut and Chinese food. The best one I have heard is the one that the famous *New York Times* correspondent Theodore White tells in his memoirs.

Chou En-lai invited Theodore White to a banquet in his honor when White was recalled to New York City. In his heart, Ted knew he had been eating non-kosher food in China, but used the "safe *treif*" rule to avoid internal conflict. He never ate pork outright. However, the centerpiece of Chou En-lai's banquet for Ted was a golden-brown, crackle-skinned, roast suckling pig.

White reports that Chou En-lai said, "*Ch'ing ch'ing,*" "Please, please," and gestured to him to break the crackle first. White explained that he was Jewish and that Jews were not allowed to eat any kind of pig. The Chinese hosts became downcast and silent because of their embarrassing faux pas. Chou then lifted his chopsticks, pointed at the pig and said, "Teddy, this is China. Look again. See. Look. It looks to you like pig. But in China, this is not a pig – this is a duck."

Everyone broke up laughing and Ted broke the crackle and ate his first mouthful of certified pig, for which he said he hoped his ancestors would forgive him. Under the circumstances, I would hope so too.

KOSHER CHINESE PRODUCTS

In this book, I include recipes that can be made according to kashrut standards that are probably acceptable to most Jews in Reform, Reconstructionist and Conservative branches. Many of the recipes should also be acceptable to more ritually observant Jews, pending decisions by their own rabbinic authorities.

I draw my kashrut standards from decisions originally made by the Asian Kashrut Society, a non-profit organization with a supervising branch office in Asia. This society provides a great deal of information on Judaic issues throughout Asia and information from them on kashrut can be found on the web at http://asiarecipe.com/kosher.html.

I make many of my Chinese sauces from scratch because it is difficult to find Chinese sauces with kosher certification. You can buy small bottles kosher soy sauce and some common "Chinese-American" sauces, such as plum sauce, in most major supermarkets. Kosher versions of more sophisticated prepared sauces; hoisin sauce, chili-garlic sauce and vegetarian oyster sauce, are more difficult to find. The Iron Chef brand of Asian sauces now sells excellent kosher hoisin and chili-garlic sauces.

When I was researching this book, I wrote to over a dozen kosher Chinese restaurants to get their sauce sources, but to no avail. Not one responded. After additional questioning, the sense I got was that the certification process for sauces made in Asia as kosher is a secret. My recommendation with respect to Chinese sauces is to search American and Asian markets in your region and check bottles for the kosher symbols – or make your own.

In my Chinese cooking, I use ingredients that can be found in large supermarkets and Asian markets. All fresh vegetables are kosher. With respect to other Chinese products, the following are the kashrut rulings by the Asian Kosher Society.

The following ingredients are kosher *without* supervision:

- All vegetables.
- Fermented black beans (salted black beans) – small fermented black beans preserved in salt, and an important ingredient in many Chinese dishes.
- Rice wine – a grain product that can be used in the kosher kitchen. A good substitute is sherry.
- Szechwan peppercorns – dried, aromatic berries with a strong, distinct aroma when roasted. They are used whole or crushed into a powder.
- Bean curd (tofu) – made from ground dried soy beans and water, to which a coagulant, gypsum powder is added to curdle the mixture.
- Water chestnuts – vegetable with crisp, white sweet flesh. The canned versions are flavorless compared to fresh ones that have

to be peeled. Jicama, a tuber that also has a crisp white flesh, is a good substitute.

- Cellophane noodles (bean threads) – dried thin noodles made from mung bean flour. They become transparent when braised, hence the name cellophane. Kosher without supervision if made with plain ingredients: water, salt, bisulphates, rice or wheat.
- Rice noodles – thin, dried rice noodles made from rice flour. Kosher without supervision if made with plain ingredients: water, salt, bisulphates, rice or wheat.
- Rice sticks – dried noodles made from rice powder.
- Egg noodles, fresh or dried – noodles made from wheat flour, eggs and water. Kosher without supervision if made with plain ingredients: water, salt, bisulphates, rice or wheat.
- Egg roll wrappers – square sheets of fresh egg noodle dough, found in the refrigerated section of supermarkets and Asian groceries. Kosher without supervision if made with plain ingredients: water, salt, bisulphates, rice or wheat.
- Spring roll wrappers – thin wheat crepes found in the refrigerated section of Chinese grocery stores. Kosher without supervision; but they have to be made with plain ingredients: water, salt, bisulphates, rice or wheat.
- Wonton wrappers – small squares of fresh egg noodle dough found in the refrigerated section of Chinese grocery stores or supermarkets. Kosher without supervision but they have to be made with plain ingredients: water, salt, bisulphates, rice or wheat.
- Shiitake mushrooms – these are the most widely-used mushrooms in Asian cooking and are grown in China and Japan on the wood of dead deciduous trees. Dried ones should be soaked in warm water for 20 minutes.
- Cinnamon – the dried, aromatic bark of an evergreen of the laurel family, native to Ceylon and India.
- Coriander – the fresh leaves and the seeds are used.

- Gingerroot – the rhizome of the plant. Sold in root, powder or pickled forms.
- Five spice powder – ground powder made with cinnamon, star anise, white pepper, salt and other spices.
- Soy sauce.

The following ingredients are kosher only *with* supervision:

- Asian sesame oil – Asian sesame oil made from roasted sesame seeds.
- Seasoned pressed bean curd – fresh bean curd pressed to remove much of the water, then simmered in soy sauce and spices.
- Vegetarian oyster sauce – a salty, thick sauce made with mock oyster extract.
- Hoisin sauce – a thick, salty, red, sweet and sour peppery sauce made with wheat, soy beans or plums.
- Chinese chili sauce – a very spicy sauce made from chili and sesame oil.

CHINESE COOKING TECHNIQUES

Chinese cookbooks usually have descriptions of a multitude of cooking techniques unique to the cuisine, and many home cooks tell me that they are "afraid" to cook Chinese style because it is so "difficult." This fear is foolish. Chinese food, like Western food, is roasted in ovens, sautéed in pans, barbequed over coals, and poached, boiled and braised in pots. The only truly different cooking techniques for Western cooks are stir-frying and steaming.

Home cooks don't even have to buy specialized Chinese tools to prepare a satisfactory Chinese meal. I once made a Chinese dinner over a wood campfire in a remote peat bog in northern Canada, where I was armed with a single cast iron frying pan, a spoon and a small Swiss army knife!

What *does* separate Chinese cooking from Western cooking is that almost all food is pre-cut before serving. If you want to cook authentic Chinese food, you do need to learn how to chop and dice – or use a food processor.

Of the two non-Western methods of cooking, Chinese stir-frying is done at a much higher heat than normal sautéing. Unless you have a commercial gas stove and a frying pan that really transmits heat very well (cast iron works well), it can be difficult to stir-fry meats and other foods properly in a standard frying pan.

Given all this, it *is* convenient to have two special Chinese cooking tools to make the cooking experience easier and more enjoyable – a decent Chinese vegetable knife and a wok. These tools can be found at any kitchen supply store or on the Internet.

GENERAL PREPARATION

I assume that most readers are familiar with the general practices of cooking, such as assembling sauce ingredients in a bowl rather than pouring them onto a plate and serving the food in nice dishes at the table and not in frying pans.

CHOPPING AND SLICING

The Chinese vegetable knife, popularized and now manufactured by most major cutlery companies as a Santoku knife, has a rectangular blade that makes it easy to slice and chop accurately.

Some cooks like to use a medium-sized French chef's knife, which works just as well if you have the skill. You can also use a kitchen processor if you want to remove your hands completely from any chance of harm. I personally find it more pleasing to cut by hand unless I am cooking for a large number of people.

The key to learning how to chop quickly and accurately is to *always* make sure that when you hold the food you *curve your fingers* away from the blade and never let the edge of the knife go above your knuckles. I repeat – *curve your fingers away from the blade*. That way, the knife's cutting edge doesn't include pieces of your fingertips or skin as the blade slides nicely along the edge of your knuckles.

Ideally, you push the food with your thumb forward toward the knife's cutting edge, *always* being aware where your thumb is located. If you try it slowly, you should get the hang of it.

It is always better to slice narrow vegetables (e.g. string beans, celery, carrots etc.) on the *slant* to increase surface area and taste.

If you want to dice a vegetable, such as squash, potato, onion or eggplant, it is prudent to make a thin slice on one side, place the vegetable sliced-side down on the cutting board to keep it stable and then make a series of cuts along the long side. Holding the cut slices together in a pile, you then cut them again into cubes. Dicing and slicing meat is easier if the meat is partially frozen.

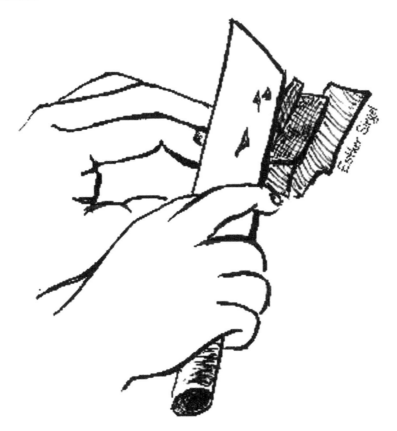

WOK COOKING

The wok is a cooking device that is a joy to use for almost all kinds of cooking, but most notably stir-frying. To stir-fry, you put a small amount of oil in a wok; quickly sauté condiments, vegetables and meats, and then add a small amount of liquid and seasonings to finish. Stir-frying takes all of about 5 minutes from start to finish.

If you buy a wok, buy the largest one that fits on your stove, and also buy a Chinese long-handled stainless steel wok spatula used to stir-fry. Ideally, the wok should also have a cover.

When stir-frying or deep oil frying in a wok or another pan, I'm often asked when I know the oil is hot enough. It's hot enough when a one-inch slice of scallion (green onion) immediately sizzles and spins about in the oil when it is tossed into it.

In my wok, I have braised meat, simmered stews, prepared soups, stir-fried almost everything, steamed fish and fried dumplings. I could put my wok into the oven and roast a chicken, and maybe even bake a cake in it. The wok is a truly remarkable cooking device. I love my wok.

STIR-FRYING

Stir-frying is easy. You can make a delicious stir-fry dish with just about anything. Sliced lamb, beef or chicken should be marinated for 15 minutes in cornstarch to prevent the meat from getting tough. Egg white can be used for fish or chicken as well. The cornstarch or egg white forms a barrier to the oil when the meat cooks.

A BASIC STIR-FRY DISH

1 pound diced or thinly-sliced
  meat, seafood or mixed
  vegetables or combination
2 teaspoons cornstarch mixed
  with 1 tablespoon water (if
  meat or fish is used)
1 teaspoon Asian sesame oil
2–3 tablespoons cooking oil
1 tablespoon minced fresh ginger
1 teaspoon minced garlic
3 scallions, sliced diagonally
  into ½-inch-long pieces
1 tablespoon cornstarch mixed
  with ¼ cup cold water

1. Marinate the meat (if used) in cornstarch and water for 15 minutes.
2. Heat the oils until very hot (a scallion sizzles in it).
3. Add the ginger and garlic and stir-fry for 15 seconds.
4. Add meat/vegetables and scallions and stir-fry until the meat is almost done and vegetables are just a little crisp. If you use both meat and vegetables, cook the meat first for 1–2 minutes and then add the vegetables and stir-fry for 1 more minute.
5. Add ¼ cup of all-purpose stir-fry sauce (see following recipe); heat until simmering, add cornstarch-water mixture and cook until the dish thickens. If too thick, add water to thin.

ALL PURPOSE STIR-FRY SAUCE

½ cup soy sauce
¼ cup chicken broth or
  vegetarian substitute
¼ cup sherry
2½ tablespoons sugar
½ tablespoon Asian sesame oil
⅛ teaspoon white pepper
1 tablespoon cooking oil
1 teaspoon each garlic and
  fresh ginger, minced

Mix all ingredients together.
This sauce keeps well for several weeks in the refrigerator.

STEAMING

Steaming is one Chinese cooking method that most Western cooks have never tried. To steam an item, you need to put it on a flat surface above boiling water in a covered container. I have an insert for my wok that is a round flat steel pan, much like a pizza pan, with holes punched in it. The pan fits about two inches above the bottom of the wok. I put the food to be steamed directly on the oiled pan or on cabbage leaves or parchment paper above boiling water in the wok, put the top on the wok, and voilà, a steamer. A pizza pan with holes punched in it would do well in a wok big enough for it.

You can cover the wok with aluminum foil if you don't have a commercial cover for it. Finally, for steamed fish and other meats, take four chopsticks and place them on the bottom of a wok so they overlap to form a wide "tic tac toe" square. Then put a dish of food on top. The food will steam above the chopsticks, which in turn will be above the boiling water.

Steaming can also be done in a large pot with some stackable bamboo or stainless steel steamers found in Asian stores or on the Internet. Put some cabbage leaves in each steamer; top them with the food being steamed; cover and stack them over an inch or so of boiling water in a large covered pot. Every few minutes, for about 8–10 minutes, rotate the steamers to make sure the food is cooked evenly. Alternatively, put a coffee cup on the bottom of the pot; place a dish on top and then steam the food on the dish. I personally like the wok method – it's easier.

THE DROP DEAD TIP FOR MAKING A CHINESE DINNER

The key to making a successful Chinese meal is organization, organization and more organization. I cut everything and organize chopped condiments (garlic, fresh ginger, hot peppers, salt, sugar, etc.) and sauces in a systematic way on my preparation table.

I place chopped and sliced meats and vegetables for each dish in a container (bowl, plate or baggies), and on top of them, little containers or plates with pre-measured herbs, spices and liquids. Then, when the cooking begins, everything goes like clockwork. This organization method works for dinners of only a few people to large banquets.

Friends ask me how long it takes to prepare a Chinese eight to ten-course banquet for 100 people. The answer, even when I make roast duck, is ten hours (with a few volunteers to help) from start to finish. The success is due to organization and discipline; getting everything ready before the guests arrive.

THE CHINESE KITCHEN CABINET

There are some essential ingredients used in Chinese cooking which I always have stocked in my house.

- Soy sauce
- Fresh ginger, cut into large pieces and stored in sherry

- Garlic heads
- Asian sesame oil
- Dried chili peppers
- Vegetarian mushroom sauce
- Hoisin sauce
- Rice wine vinegar
- Dry sherry
- Smooth peanut butter
- Dried shiitake mushrooms
- Dried Chinese chili peppers
- Five spice powder
- A good kosher canned chicken stock

With these ingredients, along with salt, pepper and sugar, you can make a wide variety of Chinese dishes.

THE KOSHER
CHINESE RECIPES

WHERE ARE THE RECIPES FROM?

I'm asked where I get all my Chinese recipes from and how I learned to cook Chinese food. To be honest, I learned Chinese cooking by eating in a lot of excellent restaurants in the great Chinatowns of Boston, San Francisco, Toronto and New York City until I knew what combinations of flavors I liked. Then I bought Chinese cookbooks and began to experiment until I was able to reproduce what I had tasted. Most of my recipes are modifications of those I've worked with.

I normally eat in little restaurants in Chinatown recommended by Chinese friends or Chinese people I ask in the street. These restaurants are filled with Asian customers. I avoid Chinese restaurants that are advertised in hotels and tourist magazines, or outrageously decorated in Chinese bric-a-brac.

As for the recipes, I try to use ones that are authentic Chinese recipes and not "Chinese-American" cooking. If followed religiously (pun intended), my recipes should always be successful. However, cooking is a craft and all cooks need to taste their food, adjusting to get the flavors that they want. Combinations of soy sauce, garlic, scallions, ginger, rice wine or sherry,

Asian sesame oil and rice wine vinegar are what make Chinese food taste "Chinese," analogous to how different combinations of garlic, onion and paprika flavor much of East European Jewish cuisine (the meat part, in any case).

Obviously, I'm not Chinese but a Jew of Eastern European decent. I never had a grandmother who made me Chinese comfort food; nor have I had formal training in Chinese cooking. Nevertheless, friends, including Asians, tell me that my food tastes authentic, and that's good enough for me.

Finally, I have tried to make all my recipes as simple as possible, using easily accessible ingredients. There may be quite a few ingredients at times; but the assembly of the dish usually is not difficult if everything is organized.

ON SEASONING

I use a bit less soy sauce than is called for in most Chinese recipes because standard soy sauce in United States markets (e.g. Kikkoman) is quite salty. I urge you to make the recipe and then taste, adding more or less soy sauce in ¼-teaspoon increments to your liking.

ON MEAT SUBSTITUTIONS

Pork is used in many Chinese dishes. Veal is the best substitute for pork because, unlike beef, it does not toughen when cooked. For those who prefer not to eat veal, turkey or dark chicken, meat is usually a good substitute. Gluten or textured vegetable protein can be substituted for meat if you are a vegetarian.

ON STIR-FRYING

Chinese cooks use more oil in their stir-frying than I do. Oil in many parts of China provides necessary calories in the diet. My Chinese dishes, therefore, are not as "rich" as their equivalents in restaurants, although they still capture the essential Chinese flavors. If you want ultra-authentic stir-fry dishes, double the oil in the recipes.

ON DEEP-FAT FRYING

Most home cooks are neither equipped nor inclined to deep fat fry food – at the very least, you have to figure out what to do with those used quarts of oil after the meal. Although I own a little deep-fat fryer, I usually "oven fry" my Chinese fried food or choose alternative cooking methods.

ON THICKENING, MARINATING AND TENDERIZING

Chinese cooks thicken their sauces with cornstarch dissolved in water at an approximate one-to-two ratio (e.g. 1 tablespoon of cornstarch in 2 tablespoons of water). I like the consistency of my sauces fairly light, something between what is found in Chinese-American restaurants and Thai restaurants. In any case, you need to cook the sauce until it becomes clear, which happens rather quickly. To thicken, make the cornstarch-water mixture and dribble it into the simmering dish, mixing, until you get the desired texture. You can use the cornstarch mixture in any recipe to thicken the sauce to the desired consistency.

Before stir-frying, dust meats and tofu with cornstarch. The cornstarch prevents the protein from getting tough during stir-frying. One easy way to dust the meat is to toss the meat with the cornstarch in a bag.

Speaking of tough meat, I find kosher beef often especially tough even after cooking. I don't use monosodium glutamate to tenderize it, though. I use ¼ teaspoon of baking soda per pound of beef. I briefly rub the baking soda into the sliced beef before I stir-fry it; or I put the baking soda into the marinade if a marinade is in the recipe. No one will develop an adverse reaction to the tenderizing process if baking soda is used.

ON RICE COOKING

Most Chinese meals at restaurants serve white rice with the food. However, I was told that rice is used as a filler at a Chinese banquet, and so I don't usually serve it unless I really have a lot of people to fill, so to speak. The Chinese prefer rice that is slightly sticky after it is cooked so it can be picked up easily with chopsticks. Long-grained rice will not cook up sticky. In contrast, short grain rice that is "squat," like little rugby balls, is better.

There are many philosophies on cooking rice, and the best way to get into an argument with Asians is to suggest a different cooking method from the one they know. I use a common rule of thumb that, for every cup of rice, add two cups of water. I boil mine, covered, for about 30 minutes or until the water is absorbed. For large banquets, I bake my rice in large covered pans, using the same ratio.

The fail-safe way to make rice is with a rice cooker, but you really don't need one if you take the time to check the rice when it is cooking, adding more water as needed. Rice cooking in a microwave boils over; so put a plate under the covered dish to catch the overflow.

PREPARING A FULL MEAL

Full Chinese meals consist of several dishes. Some people like to serve steamed or boiled rice with Chinese food. If you want a full dinner for a family, you should probably select one appetizer or dim sum; a soup; a meat, fish or tofu dish; a vegetable dish and a dessert. For multi-course dinners, it is best to prepare cold dishes and stews beforehand and only have a few stir-fry offerings. Otherwise, the cook is always in the kitchen.

CHEF'S HINTS

I recommend that you spend time composing your Chinese dishes to look as great as they taste. I often surround meat dishes with bright-green steamed Chinese vegetables and use minced red bell pepper, cilantro or scallions to sprinkle as garnish to make my food "picture perfect." The "oohs and aaahs" from your family or guests will prove me right.

At the bottom of some recipes I've put a little "Chef's Hint," my homage to Chicago chef Louis Szathmary's book *The Chef's Secret Cook Book*, in which he included recipes from the former Chicago eatery, *The Bakery*. These hints are the "secrets" in some of my dishes.

OTHER CHINESE KOSHER COOKBOOKS

There have only been a few popular kosher Chinese cookbooks. Ruth and Bob Grossman published the first, *The Chinese Kosher Cookbook*, in 1963. This cookbook consisted of recipes with names that consisted of word plays on Chinese and Yiddish, and the recipes were made with ingredients that were often a "mish-mash" of Jewish and Chinese cuisine.

For example, Foh Nee Shrimp Puffs (get it?) consisted of browning gefilte fish balls (formed balls of chopped whitefish and spices in jelly) in oil and then serving them with hot mustard and plum sauce. Another example is Far Blun Jed Egg Drop Soup ("Far Blun Jed" is a Yiddish expression meaning, "mixed up" or "lost"), which consisted of chicken soup thickened with egg and cornstarch with some watercress for appearance. This soup was indeed "mixed up" and most of the recipes in this book were rather unauthentic – although they certainly were kosher.

A second kosher Chinese cookbook is one of the most outstanding Chinese cookbooks I own: Millie Chan's *Kosher Chinese Cookbook*. Ms. Chan teaches Chinese cooking in New York City and it shows. Sadly, Chan's book is no longer in print, perhaps because she used too many ingredients that are hard to find in typical supermarkets and cooking styles (e.g. deep fat frying) that many Americans do not like to use in this health-conscious time.

汤

SOUPS

Soups are an integral part of most Chinese dinners, and are served not at the beginning, but during the meal. Essentially, the Chinese consider soup as a beverage, sometimes just a simple broth with a few vegetables poached in it. My family loves all kinds of Chinese soups. The better Chinese restaurants serve huge bowls of soup with various kinds of noodles, seafood, vegetables and meats that make a complete one-pot meal. Chicken, vegetable, beef or pork-based stocks are used to make Chinese soups.

I start the soup section of the recipe collection with these basic stocks (except of course, pork). If you don't want to take the time to make your own stock, you can buy kosher chicken broth (not soup) or powdered stock preparations. The best of the powdered preparations is the Israeli-made Osem brand soup stocks.

CHICKEN STOCK 8 servings

This stock is a wonder to eat if you have the flu or feel under the weather. It is Chinese cold therapy.

>1 slice fresh ginger, about ⅛-inch thick
>1 tablespoon Asian sesame oil
>2 quarts water
>4 pounds chicken parts
>¼ teaspoon white pepper
>1 tablespoon soy sauce or salt to taste
>2 teaspoons Asian sesame oil

1. In a pot, sauté the ginger in Asian sesame oil for 20 seconds and add 2 quarts of water and 4 pounds of chicken parts or cut-up chicken and bring to a simmer.
2. Add the white pepper, salt or soy sauce, and cook until the chicken is done, for about 1 hour. Skim off the scum that floats to the top of the pot in the first 10 minutes. Cool and remove chicken for other uses.

Chef's Hint: If you use canned chicken soup or powders, sauté the ginger as above, and then add the soup, salt and pepper. This stock, served very hot, is comfort food if you have a cold or virus.

VEGETABLE STOCK

6–8 servings

A vegetarian version of soup stock.

3 tablespoons vegetable oil
1 medium scallion, chopped
3 cups green cabbage, chopped
   into coarse cubes
1 carrot, thinly sliced
3 dried shiitake mushrooms,
   stems broken off
1 small potato, diced
1 large fennel bulb, roughly chopped
5 cups water
1 teaspoon kosher salt (coarse salt)
⅛ teaspoon white pepper

1. Heat the oil in a pot and stir-fry scallion for 1 minute.
2. Add the remaining ingredients and continue to stir-fry
   for 2–3 minutes more.
3. Add water and simmer partially covered for 1½ hours.
4. Add salt and pepper to taste. Strain and store or freeze for
   use later.

Chef's Hint: Adding one apple, peeled and diced, or 1½ cups of chopped
dates gives the soup a nice sweet undertone.

EGG DROP SOUP   4–6 servings

Egg drop soup with wontons is a favorite simple soup found in every Chinese restaurant. It is the Chinese equivalent of Jewish chicken soup.

> 4 cups chicken stock
> 2 teaspoons sherry
> 2 eggs, lightly beaten
> 1 tablespoon cornstarch mixed
>   with 2 tablespoons water
> 1–2 scallions, minced
> 1 teaspoon cilantro leaves,
>   minced (optional)

1. Bring to a simmer 4 cups of chicken stock. Add the sherry and slowly pour the eggs in a stream, stirring the soup in a circular motion for a minute or so.
2. Slowly add 1 tablespoon of cornstarch mixed with 2 of tablespoons water until the soup is thick enough for your taste. Adding ½ cup of frozen or fresh peas is a nice variation at the end, just before serving.
3. Garnish with scallion and cilantro and serve.

Chef's Hint: Adding the teaspoon of chopped cilantro leaves gives the soup a unique fresh flavor. Using only egg whites instead of whole eggs to thicken the soup will create beautiful ribbons in the soup.

SOUP WONTONS

40 dumplings

Homemade wontons, soup dumplings, are made with an egg-based noodle dough that will be familiar to any ethnic cook, from Jewish to Italian. It is marvelous that this dough is ubiquitous to so many cultures.

If you don't want to make wontons from scratch, you can buy kosher prepared wonton skins in 50-piece packages in most major supermarkets.

THE SKINS:

2–2½ cups unbleached
   all-purpose white flour
¾ teaspoon salt
1 large egg, beaten
⅓–½ cup water

1. Mix the flour and salt in a bowl and add the beaten egg, mixing the dough with your fingers. Add the water slowly, mixing and squeezing the mixture to form a dough. If the mixture falls apart, add a bit more water.
2. Remove the dough from the bowl; form into a ball and knead until it is smooth, yet soft. Coat with oil on top and bottom and let the dough rest for about 30 minutes.
3. Pinch off walnut-sized pieces and roll them out into very thin 3–4-inch diameter circles on a floured surface, a bit thicker in the middle than at the edges.

THE FILLING:

1 pound ground turkey, beef or veal
1 tablespoon minced scallion
1 teaspoon minced fresh ginger
2 tablespoons soy sauce
1 teaspoon salt

½ teaspoon sugar
1 tablespoon Asian sesame oil
2 teaspoons sherry
1 teaspoon cornstarch
1 egg
⅛ teaspoon white pepper
1 tablespoon cilantro leaves (optional)

1. Mix all the ingredients together. Take a wonton skin and place ½–1 teaspoon of the filling in the middle; fold skin over into a half moon shape and seal the edges with a bit of water; Or take a second skin and place it on top of the first one with the filling, sealing the edges with water.

2. Prepare two quarts of boiling water; turn off the heat and drop in about 20 wontons. Bring the pot to a boil again and then lower the heat to simmer the wontons for about 10 minutes. The wontons will be done when they float to the top. Drain them gently in a colander. Transfer with a slotted spoon to bowls. Repeat as necessary.

IN CHINA, Jews were allowed to build their first synagogue in 1163 during the Southern Song dynasty. During the Mongol dynasty (1279–1368 C.E.), Jews had high enough social status to be made the administrators of other Central Asian and Middle Eastern foreigners.

CORN SOUP

4–6 servings

Corn is an American food that was incorporated into Chinese-American cooking. This version of egg drop soup is often made with crab meat, but a kosher version of mock seafood, known as surimi, is an acceptable substitute. My recipe is modified from one given to me by Marjory Hsiang. I add peas for color and sherry for taste.

4 cups chicken stock
½ cups surimi or mock shrimp,
   shredded (optional)
1½ cups frozen corn
2 teaspoons sherry
1 egg, lightly beaten
1 tablespoon cornstarch mixed
   with 2 tablespoons water
1–2 scallions, minced
1 tablespoon frozen peas
1 teaspoon minced cilantro
   leaves (optional)

1. Bring to a simmer 4 cups of chicken stock.
2. Add the corn and seafood and bring back to a simmer.
3. Add the sherry and slowly pour the egg in a stream, stirring the soup in a circular fashion for a minute or so.
4. Slowly add 1 tablespoon of cornstarch mixed with 2 tablespoons of water until the soup is thick enough for your taste. Add scallions, peas and cilantro, and serve.

HOT SOUR SOUP   4–6 servings

American taste in Chinese food in the 1980s changed to the spicier western Szechwan and Hunan styles of cooking. Out of these styles comes this favorite soup.

3–4 dried shiitake mushrooms,
  soaked in water until soft
¼ pound thinly-sliced or diced chicken,
  beef or vegetarian wheat gluten
1 pound medium-firm to firm tofu
5 cups chicken stock
1 cup mushroom soaking liquid
1 tablespoon sherry
2 tablespoons white distilled
  or rice wine vinegar
¾ teaspoon salt
1 teaspoon soy sauce
¼–½ teaspoon white pepper
several drops Asian sesame oil
1 egg, beaten
2 tablespoons cornstarch
  mixed with ¼ cup water
1 scallion, minced

1. Add everything to a large pot except the egg, cornstarch-water mixture and scallion, and bring to a boil. Simmer for 5 minutes.
2. Slowly add the egg to the simmering soup, stirring in a circular motion to make egg shreds. Then add the cornstarch mixture to thicken and the scallions to garnish. Adjust with more pepper or vinegar to taste.

CHRYSANTHEMUM HOT POT   6–8 servings

During the winter, there is almost nothing my family and guests love more than a Chinese hot pot dinner. Chicken or another broth simmers in a pot located between diners, who spear pre-cut pieces of raw food, poach them in the broth, dip them in a sauce, and then eat them hot. I sometimes do the poaching in the kitchen and bring out platters of the poached meats and vegetables to the table. The Chinese hot pot has a long history. It originated in cold northern China where beef and mutton were added to the pot and the style then spread to other regions. I've used electric skillets, fondue pots and "fry-baby" deep-fat fryers to make a hot pot at the table.

The flavor of the soup changes, depending on what proportions of food you put into it. Every soup is different. People who don't follow kashrut often add seafood. I made a Hot Pot Soup as a course in a recent banquet for 120 people, keeping the poached food *in* the soup. It was a smash hit.

The cooked food is dipped into dumpling dipping sauce, scallions ground with salt (see Chef's Hint), and hoisin sauce thinned with some water.

2 quarts Chinese chicken stock
2 whole chicken breasts and
 ½ pound beef, sliced ⅛-inch thick
1–2 pounds spinach, washed
½ head Chinese cabbage and/or
 bok choy, cut into 2-inch pieces
1 pound white firm-fleshed fish
 instead of shrimp and scallops
 (e.g. swordfish, monkfish or
 halibut), cut into 1-inch pieces
¼ pound thin rice noodles
1 pound extra firm tofu, cut
 into 1-inch cubes
1 bunch scallions, trimmed

½ pound button, fresh
   shiitake or portabella
   mushrooms, cut into 1-inch pieces
several eggs, beaten
1 large white chrysanthemum
   blossom (optional)
1 tablespoon chopped coriander
2 cups cooked white rice

1. Give diners some of each ingredient. After they poach the food, and eat it fondue style, poach eggs or pour the beaten eggs into the communal soup pot to create egg ribbons.
2. Serve the soup in individual bowls with some flower petals over ¼ cup of cooked white rice.

Chef's Hint: A dynamite dipping powder for the poached meats is made by grinding together ½ cup of non-iodized salt and 4 scallions (green and white parts) in a blender for one minute.

OUR ANCESTORS came to this land from the northwest nearly three thousand years ago, and had with them a roll of the law that was very ancient and in a language that we do not understand today, because we have no teachers.

    –An interviewed Kaifeng Jew, reported by Oliver Bainbridge,
    National Geographic Magazine, October, 1907.

WEST LAKE SOUP
4–6 servings

Everyone knows about egg drop soup, but how about trying the same thing with beef? Such is the delicious West Lake Soup.

⅔ cup lean ground beef or
   vegetarian meat substitute
4–5 cups chicken stock
   or vegetarian stock
1 teaspoon sugar
¼ teaspoon pepper
salt to taste
2 egg whites, lightly beaten
1½ tablespoons cornstarch mixed
   with 3 tablespoons water to
   thicken soup (optional)
2 scallions, minced
dash vinegar

BEEF MARINADE
1 tablespoon soy sauce
1 tablespoon dry sherry
1 tablespoon cornstarch
¼ teaspoon salt

1. Mix the marinade ingredients together and marinate the beef for 10 minutes.
2. Bring the chicken stock to a boil and stir in the beef. Add the sugar and pepper and simmer for 5 more minutes.
3. Slowly pour in the egg whites as with egg drop soup, stirring in a circular motion. Garnish with scallions; sprinkle with a bit of vinegar and serve.

BANQUET SOUP

4–6 servings

This is an unusual soup because it has tomato and creamed corn, which were introduced to China from the Americas. It is a favorite banquet soup that I serve.

¼ pound fresh tomatoes

13 medium fresh mushrooms

¼ pound snow pea pods, bok
  choy or Chinese broccoli

2 tablespoons vegetable oil

2 tablespoons sherry

4 cups chicken broth

½ teaspoon sugar

1 teaspoon Asian sesame oil

1 can creamed corn

2 tablespoons cornstarch dissolved
  in 4 tablespoons water

1 large egg white, beaten

⅛ cup chopped cilantro leaves

salt or soy sauce to taste

1. Coarsely chop the tomatoes, mushrooms and vegetables
    and sauté briefly in vegetable oil.
2. Add sherry, chicken broth, sugar and Asian sesame oil
    and bring to a simmer.
3. Add the creamed corn and cornstarch mixture and
    simmer until slightly thickened.
4. Dribble the egg white into the simmering soup and add
    cilantro at the end. Salt to taste.

早茶

APPETIZERS (DIM SUM)

One of my favorite restaurant experiences is to have brunch in a Chinese restaurant specializing in dim sum. Dim sum are Chinese appetizers, small morsels that come wheeled out on carts. Patrons select what they want to eat from the carts; each portion is small so many can be sampled at a table of people. A dim sum meal is similar to a Spanish "tapas" meal – you get to taste many items from salty to sweet, crispy to succulent, for an extended period of time. Appetizers are a favorite part of all my Chinese meals.

Chinese appetizers range from the familiar chicken wings and egg rolls to the less familiar fried and steamed dumplings, spring rolls, filled buns, flat breads and savory crepes.

CHICKEN WINGS

The Chinese are more adventurous eaters than most Westerners. They love eating chicken wings and duck feet and other animal parts that Americans don't often try. Fried chicken wings are one exception, perhaps because of the influence of the Anchor Bar in Buffalo, New York, which popularized "Buffalo" chicken wings as bar food decades ago.

Restaurant Chinese chicken wings are deep-fat fried in vegetable oil and then sauced later. However, many home cooks don't do much deep-fat frying in these health-conscious days. I roast my chicken wings in the oven, a cooking process that is an excellent substitute for the deep-fat fried versions.

WINGS KARPER   3–4 servings

I don't know where our friend Marcia Karper found this recipe, which has a distinctly Chinese-American thick, sticky and salty sweet sauce, but it is really good!

2–3 pounds chicken wings, separated
    into mini-drumsticks and winglets
⅛–¼ cup vegetable oil

MARINADE:
    6 tablespoons brown sugar
    6 tablespoons soy sauce
    ½ cup sherry
    ⅓ cup water
    ¼ teaspoon garlic powder or
        1 clove garlic, finely chopped

1. Line a baking sheet with aluminum foil and oil well. Place the wings on the sheet. Mix the marinade and pour it over the wings. Bake at 475°F for 30 minutes.
2. Turn wings over and bake for another 30 minutes or until they are dark and caramelized.

Chef's Hint: The sugar caramelizes on the wings, making them special. Make sure you oil the aluminum foil very well to prevent the wings from sticking.

SOY WINGS

6–8 servings

This is an authentic Chinese chicken wing recipe, not as sweet as the Karper version.

3½–4 pounds chicken wings, separated
　　into mini-drumsticks and winglets
⅛–¼ cup vegetable oil

MARINADE:
1¼ cups soy sauce
1¼ cups sherry
1 cup water
12 whole scallions, ends trimmed,
　crushed with the side of a knife
1 head garlic, cloves peeled and
　crushed with the side of a knife
2½-inch slice fresh ginger, peeled,
　cut into 10 slices, ⅛-inch thick,
　crushed with the side of a knife

1. Place the marinade ingredients in a saucepan. Heat until boiling and simmer for 10 minutes. Coat the wings with the marinade. Cover and let the wings sit in the refrigerator for several hours or overnight.
2. Preheat the oven to 475°F. Line a baking sheet with aluminum foil. Grease foil and arrange the wings on the baking sheets. Brush liberally with the marinade.
3. Roast for about 45–60 minutes, turning once, until the wings are cooked and crispy brown at the edges.

PEANUT WINGS

6–8 servings

Peanut butter goes well with wings.

3½–4 pounds chicken wings, separated
  into mini-drumsticks and winglets
⅛–¼ cup vegetable oil

MARINADE:
½ cup soy sauce
3 tablespoons honey
3 cloves garlic, crushed
¼ cup sherry
⅓ cup ketchup
3 tablespoons peanut butter
⅓ cup sugar
½ teaspoon five spice powder

1. Combine all the marinade ingredients and pour over the chicken. Marinate for several hours or overnight.
2. Preheat the oven to 475°F. Line a baking sheet with aluminum foil, grease with oil and arrange the wings on the baking sheet. Do not crowd. Brush liberally with the marinade.
3. Roast for 45–60 minutes, turning once, until the wings are cooked and crispy brown at the edges.

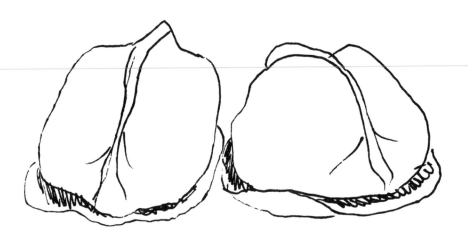

DUMPLINGS

Chinese-style dumplings are my most popular appetizers. At home I make them 50 at a time, and freeze them for snacks later. There are many styles of Chinese dumplings. You can buy wonton skins, which are round, thin flour skins; or you can make them yourself.

I first discuss how to make the dumpling skins, then how to make different dumpling shapes, and finally present a series of dumpling fillings.

DUMPLING SKINS

20–30 dumplings

2½ cups unsifted flour
1 cup cold water
½ teaspoon salt

1. Mix together ingredients and knead until smooth (you can do this in a mixer if you wish). Let rest for 15 minutes and then, on a floured surface, shape into a long rope about 12 inches long and 1 inch in diameter. Pinch off walnut-sized pieces.

2. Flatten each piece with your hand to form a thin, round pancake approximately 3 inches in diameter and roll out to 1/16-inch thick. The center should be slightly thicker than the edges. Make sure the skins are floured lightly to prevent them from sticking.

Chef's Hint: Homemade skins are much easier to seal than commercial ones, and much tastier too. Once you get the knack of it, making 50 homemade skins doesn't take too much time and is well worth the effort. It's a great activity for kids, too.

MAKING DUMPLINGS

TRADITIONAL PLEATED-STYLE DUMPLINGS

Pleated, semi-circular dumplings are the most common kind of dumpling offered in Chinese restaurants.

1. Put about 2 teaspoons of filling on one side of a circular wonton skin. Fold skin over into a half-moon shape, sealing the edges with either some beaten egg or water.
2. While holding the dumpling lengthwise, curved side up, use your index finger and thumb to pinch the edges of the dough on one side of the dumpling into "pleats," pressing each pleat against the flat side of the dough to seal the dumpling as you go.

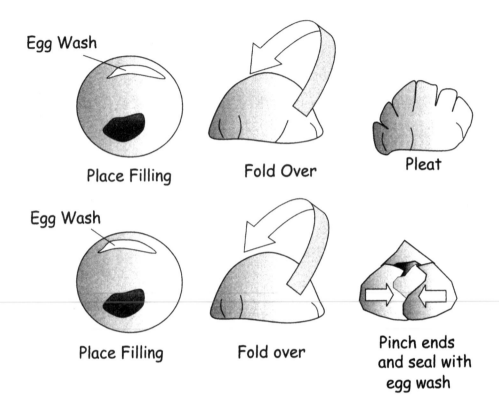

Egg Wash — Place Filling Fold Over Pleat

Egg Wash — Place Filling Fold over Pinch ends and seal with egg wash

TORTELLINI-STYLE DUMPLINGS

1. Place the filling on one side of the skin.
2. Fold over the wonton skin with the filling into a half moon.
3. Take the ends and bring them together, sealing them so they touch on the outside of the dumpling. In the process, the dumpling opens up at the top and you can see the filling (which means you can't boil them, but only steam them or make them like pot stickers).

BUNDLE-STYLE DUMPLINGS

1. Place the filling in the middle of the dumpling and fold edges and pinch at top.
2. Fold and pinch the sides together.

COOKING DUMPLINGS

Pot Stickers (frying and steaming)

---

1. In a nonstick frying pan or wok with a cover (a pizza pan works ok), heat 4 tablespoons of vegetable oil until a piece of scallion sizzles when placed in the pan.
2. Place the dumplings, crimped side up, in the wok and fry until the dumpling bottom is golden brown, for about ½ minute.
3. Pour ½ cup of water into the frying pan; cover and cook until the water is almost evaporated. Take out the dumplings and repeat the cooking process for the remaining dumplings. You may have to clean the frying pan now and then.

SIMMERING

1. Bring a large pot of water to a boil, and then lower the heat until the water bubbles in a simmer. Gently lower pleated dumplings into the water and simmer for approximately 3–5 minutes. The dumplings are cooked when the skins are translucent and the dumplings float for about 2 minutes.
2. Remove the dumplings from the pot carefully with a slotted spoon.

STEAMING

1. Place the dumplings on Chinese or American cabbage leaves set in a steamer.
2. Steam for 5–8 minutes until the dumplings are translucent.

BASIC DUMPLING SAUCE

The savory dipping sauces served with dumplings and Chinese steamed breads "make" the dish. The most popular dipping sauces are a combination of vinegar, soy sauce, water, brown sugar, garlic, hot pepper, chopped scallions and coriander leaves. I usually start with the following and then add more or fewer ingredients to taste for my "basic" dipping sauce:

> ½ cup soy sauce
> ½ cup water
> ⅛ to ¼ cup white distilled,
>   balsamic or rice wine vinegar
> 2 cloves garlic, peeled and chopped
> ¼ cup brown sugar
> 1 tablespoon Asian sesame oil
> ¼ cup chopped cilantro leaves
> 2 scallions, chopped on the diagonal
> ½ teaspoon hot pepper flakes

Chef's Hint: You need to taste when you make a dipping sauce until you get the flavor you like. Soy sauces are more or less salty, and vinegars have differing pungency. Dunk a cooked dumpling into the sauce to check the flavor.

HUNAN-STYLE DUMPLINGS   enough for 40 dumplings

This recipe is modified from the most popular appetizer at Chef Henry Chung's famous Hunan Chinese restaurant in San Francisco.

FILLING:

2 cups chopped napa cabbage

¾ pound ground beef, chicken, or veal

¼ cup scallions, minced

1 teaspoon minced fresh ginger

1 tablespoon white wine

1 egg, beaten

1 teaspoon white pepper

2 tablespoons soy sauce

1 tablespoon Asian sesame oil

1. Sprinkle a bit of salt on the chopped napa cabbage and let it sit for 30 minutes. Squeeze out the rendered water with your hands.
2. Add remaining ingredients and use as a dumpling filling.

Chef's Hint: The Chinese prefer the dark meat of the chicken to the white because dark meat has more flavor and the fat in the dark meat prevents it from drying out. I almost always use dark chicken meat in my appetizers for this reason.

VEGETARIAN DUMPLINGS   enough for 40 dumplings

My banquet patrons love vegetarian dumplings, which are also terrific as wontons or *kreplach* in soup.

FILLING:

½ pound bok choy, chopped
4 dried shiitake mushrooms
1 ounce dried cellophane noodles
¼ pound extra firm tofu or
   dried tofu (optional)
2 tablespoons Asian sesame oil
1 teaspoon salt
1 teaspoon grated fresh ginger

1. Sprinkle a bit of salt on the chopped bok choy and let it sit for 30 minutes. Squeeze out the rendered water with your hands and discard.
2. Put the mushrooms in a small bowl. Add boiling water, cover and let sit until softened (for 30 minutes). Drain. Remove the stems and finely dice; then squeeze out the water with your hands.
3. In another pot, boil the water and add noodles. Turn off heat and let sit for a few minutes to soften. Drain, chop and add to the mushrooms and bok choy.
4. Finely dice tofu and add sesame oil, salt and ginger to chopped mushrooms and bok choy to make the filling.

Chef's Hint: Use dried shiitake mushrooms, not fresh. They are the secret "meaty" ingredient that makes these dumplings so delicious. Squeezing out the water prevents the dumplings from getting soggy inside.

SPICY DUMPLINGS WITH SESAME SAUCE

enough for 40 dumplings

This is a modification of a recipe that Chef Simon Teng published in *New York's Master Chefs*.

FILLING:

2 tablespoons water

1 tablespoon finely chopped scallion

1 tablespoon finely chopped
   fresh ginger

½ pound ground veal, dark
   chicken meat or beef

¼ teaspoon salt

⅛ teaspoon ground Szechwan
   peppercorns or white pepper

SAUCE:

⅓ cup plus 1 tablespoon tahini
   (sesame seed paste) or peanut butter

⅓ cup balsamic or rice wine vinegar

¼ cup soy sauce

¼ cup sugar

1½ tablespoons Asian sesame oil

1 tablespoon finely chopped garlic

½–1 tablespoon hot chili oil or
   ½ teaspoon chili pepper flakes

½ teaspoon ground Szechwan
   peppercorns or white pepper

sliced scallions for garnish

1. Mix all the filling ingredients together.
2. Mix the sauce ingredients together and serve with dumplings.

Chef's Hint: Always use ground Szechwan peppercorns or white pepper if you can in Chinese recipes. They give a unique floral aroma that black pepper does not. This sauce is also good with vegetarian dumplings.

OUR ANCESTORS always washed their hands except the chief rabbi who entered the "House of Heaven" [a little square room, which none but the rabbi can enter during the time of prayer]. In the "House of Heaven" the rolls of the law were kept in silken curtains, and on the western wall the Ten Commandments were written in large golden letters.

–An interviewed Kaifeng Jew, reported by Oliver Bainbridge,
National Geographic Magazine, October, 1907.

SEAFOOD DUMPLINGS enough for 40 dumplings

Seafood dumplings normally use wonton skins made from rice powder, but standard wheat wontons are completely satisfactory. The filling is usually shrimp; but the kosher version below uses a fish fillet – monkfish and sea bass are particularly good. Alternatively, kosher mock shrimp, or mock seafood called surimi, can be used.

FILLING:

½ pound fish fillet, coarsely chopped

1 teaspoon grated fresh ginger

1 clove garlic, minced

½ cup finely chopped scallions

¼ cup finely chopped water chestnuts

2 tablespoons shredded carrot

1 tablespoon sherry

1 egg white

1 tablespoon Asian sesame oil

2 tablespoons chopped coriander leaves

1. Fry the ginger and garlic briefly in oil.
2. Add to the fish and remaining ingredients to make the filling.

SOUP-FILLED JUICY DUMPLINGS

enough for 30 dumplings

Imagine biting into a small steamed dumpling to find soup *inside* it. These are incredible treats worth the effort.

FILLING:
¾ pound beef, veal, chicken or
   turkey, coarsely chopped
2 teaspoons soy sauce
1 tablespoon Asian sesame oil
2 tablespoons chopped scallion greens
1½ teaspoons fresh ginger,
   finely chopped
6 tablespoons water
¼ cup stiff aspic*
basic yeast dough

1. Mix all the ingredients above for the filling.

*MAKING THE ASPIC:
1½ cups chicken broth
1 envelope gelatin

1. Boil 1 cup of broth uncovered for about 2 minutes (reducing it quite a bit).
2. Stir 1 envelope of gelatin into the other ½ cup of broth.
3. Mix together the boiled broth and the broth with gelatin and stir over a low heat until all the gelatin is dissolved.
4. Chill to make stiff aspic, enough for three recipes of this dim sum.

MAKING THE DUMPLINGS:

1. Make a recipe of homemade dumpling dough (commercial dough will not work).
2. Roll out rounds of dough 2 inches across and about ⅛-inch thick, thinner on the outside than in the middle.
3. Put 1 teaspoon of filling in the middle of the dough round. Press the edges together, twisting the top in a decorative pattern, making sure to seal well.
4. If holes appear, patch them at once! Put each dumpling on a square of waxed paper or a piece of napa leaf and steam for 8 minutes. Serve hot.

Chef's Hint: Make sure your guests pop the entire dumpling into their mouths before they bite down! You must make homemade dumpling dough for this dumpling, or the seal will not take.

IN 1903 the *New York Times* described Chinatown clientele: "It is the men and women who like to eat after everybody else is abed that pour shekels into the coffers of the man who knows how to make chop suey." Shekels. What an interesting currency to have gratuitously cited.

–Gish Jen, A Short History of the Chinese Restaurant
From stir-fried buffalo to Matzoh Foo Young,
Reported by Gish Jen in Slate, April 27, 2005,
http://slate.msn.com/id/2117567

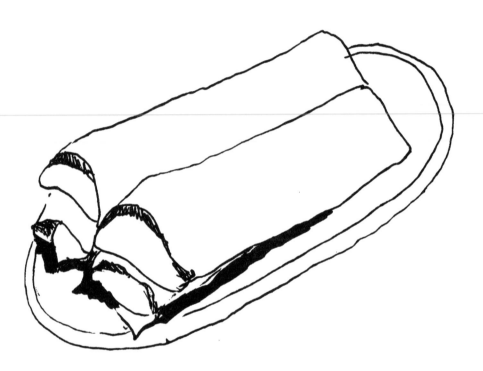

SPRING ROLLS AND EGG ROLLS

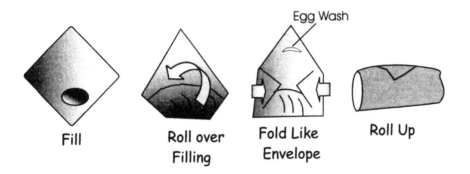

Egg Wash

Fill   Roll over Filling   Fold Like Envelope   Roll Up

Egg rolls are a mainstay appetizer in Chinese-American restaurants, where they are often made with a rather thick wheat skin that bubbles when it is fried. I prefer thinner skins, called spring roll skins or "lumpia" wrappers. I first discuss how to make the rolls, and then follow with various fillings.

1. Take the rectangular skin and orient it so it looks like a diamond.
2. Place about 1–2 tablespoons of your choice of the following fillings onto the corner nearest you and then tightly roll away from you a couple of turns.
3. Fold the side corners toward the middle to seal the ends

and make a cylinder. Keep rolling until the end. Brush some egg-water wash (1 egg beaten with 1–2 tablespoons water) on the last part of the skin to form a seal.

4. Heat oil in a wok or deep fryer to 400°F (a slice of scallion will literally "spin" wildly when you put it in the oil at that temperature), and fry the egg rolls until they are golden brown.

A SHORT distance from this (Jewish) temple I found an old, long, narrow stone in the side of an empty mud hut, which bore traces of an inscription dealing with a "Foreign heaven chapel," in which the foreigners that "pluck the sinews" fast and weep together.

–Reported by Oliver Bainbridge,
National Geographic Magazine, October, 1907

VEGETARIAN SPRING ROLL 25 spring or egg roll wrappers

Guests love my vegetarian spring rolls, the filling for which I make depending on my mood and what is available in the supermarket. Be inventive and find a combination you like among cabbages, carrots, assorted mushrooms, bamboo shoots and water chestnuts.

FILLING:
- 2 teaspoons Asian sesame oil
- 2 teaspoons minced fresh ginger
- 1 tablespoon minced garlic
- 2 dry shiitake mushrooms, softened and shredded
- 2 scallions chopped
- ½ cup grated carrots
- 2 cups shredded napa cabbage, bok choy or American cabbage
- 1 tablespoon sherry
- 2 teaspoons sugar
- 2 tablespoons soy sauce
- ¼ teaspoon white pepper
- ½ teaspoon cornstarch

1. Heat 2 teaspoons of Asian sesame oil and stir-fry the ginger and garlic for 1 minute.
2. Mix with the remaining filling ingredients.

Chef's Hint: You can replace half the bok choy or cabbage with ground beef, chicken or veal, stir-fried in 2 tablespoons of oil until slightly pink, for a non-vegetarian version.

MEAT AND NOODLE SPRING ROLL

25 spring roll wrappers

When I lived in Minneapolis, Minnesota, I had my first Vietnamese spring roll at the Phoenix Restaurant in St. Paul, which served the best Indochinese-style spring roll I've ever eaten. Indochinese cooking uses nuoc mam, a non-kosher fish sauce, instead of soy sauce. I find that soy sauce works fine.

Purists will argue that I shouldn't put a Vietnamese recipe in a Chinese cookbook; but this spring roll really shares much in common with the spring rolls I've had in some Chinese restaurants. What *is* different is the dipping sauce, which has a tangy lime component.

FILLING:

1 pound ground beef or turkey
   (vegetarian soy substitute
   works well too)
½ cup chopped onion
1 tablespoon Asian sesame oil
1½ cups shredded carrot
3 oz. bean threads, soaked in warm
   water and cut into 2-inch long pieces
3 eggs
¼ cup soy sauce
1 teaspoon garlic powder or
   3 cloves garlic, minced
1 teaspoon white pepper

1. Stir-fry the meat and onion for 1 minute in oil.
2. Mix with remaining fresh ingredients and make into rolls.
3. Deep-fry until golden brown.

DIPPING SAUCE:
  1½ inch red dried chili
  2 cloves garlic, mashed
  4 teaspoons sugar
  ¼ cup soy sauce
  2 tablespoons lime juice
  ¼ cup water
  1 tablespoon chopped coriander leaves

Mix all the ingredients together.

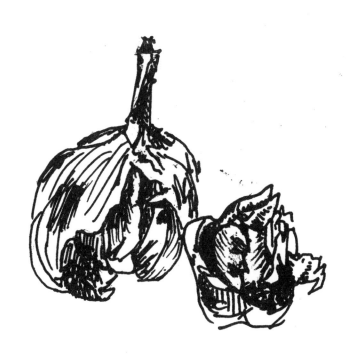

BUNS

The Chinese are parsimonious with cooking fuel and do not bake food except in big restaurants. Instead, breads are steamed or pan-fried. Instead of making the dough from scratch, you can make commercial white pizza dough or bread dough. In this sequence of bun recipes, I first instruct you how to make the dough and how to cook the buns. I then give several filling variations.

Basic Dumpling Dough

1 cup lukewarm water
1 package yeast
2–3 cups flour
2 teaspoons salt
1 tablespoon vegetable oil

1. Mix the yeast in the water and let sit for a few minutes so the yeast proofs (softens and bubbles). Add flour and salt and knead until you have a smooth, elastic, soft dough.
2. Oil the dough and place in bowl. Let rise until doubled in size for about 2 hours. Punch down.
3. To make the buns, pinch off walnut-sized pieces of dough. Flour the balls and flatten with your hand.
4. Roll it out on a floured surface until it is about 3 inches in diameter.
5. Take 1–2 teaspoons of filling of choice and then enclose it in the dough, twisting the top of the bun to seal.
6. Let rise for 15 minutes before steaming or baking.

Steamed Buns (The Traditional Way)

1. Place the buns about 1 inch apart in a steamer on cabbage leaves or on a greased steamer tray in a wok. Let rise for 15 minutes.
2. Pour 1–2 inches of water in the wok. Cover and bring to a boil.
3. Steam the buns for 5 minutes until they rise and look translucent and shiny.

Place Filling

Fold edges up

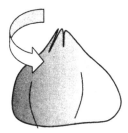

Twist at top to seal

Baked Buns

Former Chef Sum Yu of the Asia Garden Chinese restaurant in San Francisco came up with a baked version of steamed buns. This is my modification of his recipe.

GLAZE:

2 tablespoons warm water

2 teaspoons sugar or honey

1 teaspoon vegetable oil

1. Make or buy yeast dough.
2. Fill the buns with filling of choice.
3. Place the buns twisted side up, on an oiled baking pan.
4. Cover and let rise for 15 minutes.
5. Glaze with the water-sugar-oil glaze.
6. Preheat oven to 450°F.
7. Bake buns for 10 minutes until the tops are golden brown.

Pan-Fried Pot Sticker Buns

Pan-frying the buns makes them crusty on the bottom and succulent inside. Let them cool a bit before biting into them!

1. Make or buy yeast dough.
2. Fill the buns with filling of choice.
3. Heat 1 tablespoon of oil in a frying pan. Place the buns, twisted side up, so they do not touch.
4. Fry the buns until they are brown on the bottom for about 1 minute.
5. Add ¾ cup of water to the pan and cover immediately. Cook for about 6 minutes until the water has evaporated; remove the cover and cook until a crust forms on the bottom of the buns.

IN THE ancient Chinese Jewish community of Kaifeng, Jewish lineage was patrimonial, rather than matrimonial.

CHICKEN-FILLED BUNS   enough for 30 buns

One recipe basic steamed bun dough

FILLING:

½ pound raw chicken, minced
10 dried and softened shiitake
  mushrooms, shredded
¼ pound bok choy or
  ¼ pound kale, chopped
1 scallion, minced
1 tablespoon Asian sesame oil
1 tablespoon soy sauce
1 teaspoon sherry
1 tablespoon minced fresh ginger
1 teaspoon salt
¼ teaspoon pepper

1. Stir-fry the chicken until just before pinkness is lost. Add
    the remaining ingredients.
2. Fill and cook the buns.

Chef's Hint: You can add 2 tablespoons of hoisin sauce to the filling to make
a barbequed chicken-filled bun.

MUSHROOM CASHEW BUNS
enough for 30 buns

Many friends tell me that this steamed dumpling is their favorite appetizer.

One recipe basic steamed bun dough

FILLING:

¼ cup chopped mushrooms
1 small onion, chopped
1 clove garlic, chopped
1 teaspoon minced fresh ginger
½ cup chopped bamboo shoots
¾ cup chopped cashews
2 scallions, chopped

2 tablespoons vegetable oil

1. Sauté the filling mixture in oil for 3 minutes and add:

3 tablespoons soy sauce
1 tablespoon sherry
1 teaspoon sugar
¼ cup water
1 tablespoon cornstarch

2. Cool the filling. Fill the buns, seal and cook.

BARBEQUED MEAT BUNS
enough for 30 buns

Sweet-salty steamed barbequed pork buns are a staple of dim sum restaurants and street vendors. Here is a kosher version modified from Millie Chan's book.

One recipe basic steamed bun dough

FILLING:

2 tablespoons vegetable oil
1 cup diced onion
1 garlic clove, chopped
4 tablespoons soy sauce
2 tablespoons white sugar
1 tablespoon brown sugar
1 teaspoon Asian sesame oil
¼ teaspoon five spice
  powder (optional)
3 tablespoons cornstarch mixed
  with 6 tablespoons water
2 cups chopped Cantonese-
  style or plain roast turkey
½ cup minced scallions

1. Heat the oil and stir-fry the onion and garlic until transparent and add the remaining filling ingredients, except the cornstarch mixture, meat and scallions.
2. Heat to a slight boil and add the cornstarch mixture to thicken.
3. Add the meat and scallions.
4. Fill and cook the buns.

Chef's Hint: Try diced extra firm tofu for a vegetarian version.

CURRY BUNS

enough for 30 buns

Chinese cooks make curry interesting by adding ginger and soy sauce to the Indian culinary template of spices.

FILLING:

1 teaspoon Asian sesame oil

1 tablespoon vegetable oil

2 medium red onions, diced

1 tablespoon curry powder
   (Madras is especially good)

1 tablespoon minced fresh ginger

2 tablespoons vegetable oil

½ pound chicken, beef, veal
   or lamb, chopped

2 teaspoons soy sauce

1 cup frozen peas

SAUCE:

½ cup chicken broth

1½ teaspoons sugar

1 teaspoon salt

1 tablespoon cornstarch

1. Heat the sesame oil and 1 tablespoon of vegetable oil. Sauté the onions, curry powder and ginger and place in a bowl.
2. Heat 2 tablespoons of vegetable oil and sauté the meat. Add onions, peas and sauce ingredients.
3. Fill the buns and bake at 450ºF for 20 minutes until golden.

ASSORTED DIM SUM

There are many dim sum other than the traditional buns, spring rolls and dumplings. Here is an assortment.

ONION CAKES

20 *cakes*

Onion cakes are pan-fried, scallion-filled, rounds of pastry, served with dipping sauces.

2½ cups unsifted flour
1 cup cold water
½ teaspoon salt
1 tablespoon Asian sesame oil
2 scallions, minced
⅛ teaspoon salt
¼ cup vegetable oil

1. Mix together the flour, water and salt and knead until smooth. Let rest for 15 minutes and then, on a floured surface, shape into a ball.
2. Flatten into a disk and roll out to 10 inches in diameter.
3. Spread the Asian sesame oil on the disk. Sprinkle on the scallions and salt and roll into a tight rope.
4. Coil the rope into the shape of a snail's shell and pinch the end into the coil.
5. Dust with flour and roll out again into a 10-inch disk, ¼-inch thick.
6. Heat ¼ cup of vegetable oil in a frying pan or wok until a scallion sizzles in it, and then fry the onion cake on both sides until it is brown. Cut into wedges and serve with a basic dipping sauce.

P.F. CHANG'S LETTUCE WRAPS 10–15 wraps

P.F. Chang's Chinese restaurant chain is well known for these wraps. The contrast of the crunch of icy cold lettuce with the hot savory filling is wonderful.

FILLING:

    5 tablespoons vegetable oil
    1 ½ pounds boneless, skinless
        chicken, cut into ¼-inch cubes
    1 teaspoon minced fresh ginger
    2 cloves garlic, minced
    2 scallions, minced
    8 dried shiitake mushrooms,
        softened and shredded
    1 (8 ounces) can bamboo
        shoots, minced
    1 (8 ounces) can water
        chestnuts, minced
    2 small dried chilies, minced (optional)

SAUCE

    ¼ cup sugar
    ¼ cup water mixed with
        1 tablespoon cornstarch
    2 tablespoons soy sauce
    2 tablespoons rice wine vinegar
    2 tablespoons ketchup
    1 tablespoon lemon juice
    ⅛ teaspoon Asian sesame oil
    2 teaspoons Chinese hot mustard

2 teaspoons water
1–3 teaspoons garlic powder
1 teaspoon Asian sesame oil
1 teaspoon hoisin sauce
4–5 iceberg or bibb lettuce cups

1. Heat 3 tablespoons of oil in a wok and sauté the chicken breasts until no longer pink.
2. Remove the chicken from the pan. Add the remaining 2 tablespoons oil and stir-fry the garlic, ginger and scallions for 1 minute.
3. Add the remaining filling vegetables and stir-fry for 1 minute.
4. Add the chicken and sauce.
5. To prepare the lettuce leaves, place the lettuce head stem down on a table. Cut horizontally across the top of the head, about ⅓ of the way down. The leaves will separate nicely like little skullcaps. Slice the head vertically down the center, stem down. The leaves will separate nicely again into more oval-shaped pieces.
6. Mix the sauce ingredients together, stirring well.
7. Assemble the lettuce wraps by spooning 2 tablespoons of the meat and vegetable mixture into a lettuce cup.

Chef's Hint: Use tofu instead of chicken for a vegetarian version.

PAPER-WRAPPED CHICKEN   30 pieces

This is a popular appetizer where everyone gets a little packet to open to get at the morsels inside.

MARINADE:

    3 tablespoons soy sauce
    1-inch slice fresh ginger, shredded
    1 tablespoon Asian sesame oil
    1 tablespoon sherry
    3 teaspoons sugar
    ½ teaspoon five spice powder

FILLING:

    2 pounds skinless, boneless
        chicken breasts
    3–4 dried shiitake mushrooms,
        softened, thinly sliced
    3–4 scallions, sliced on diagonal
    24 sprigs cilantro (coriander leaves)
    24 6-inch squares of parchment
        paper or aluminum foil
    oil for deep-frying

1. Mix together the ingredients for marinade.
2. Cut the chicken into thin slices, roughly 2 ½ inches long, and marinate for 1 hour.
3. Take a 6-inch square of aluminum foil or parchment paper and lay it out so that it forms a diamond shape in front of you. Add 2 of the chicken slices, 1 slice of mushroom, 2 slices of scallion and a coriander sprig in

the middle, making sure to keep the filling in the center
and not near the edges.

5. Bring the bottom corner of the diamond up over the
   chicken.

6. Fold the right corner over toward the middle, then the
   left corner, so that one corner overlaps the other.

7. Roll up the section of the foil that contains the chicken,
   and then tuck the corner into the flap. It is very
   important to make sure that the packets are well sealed
   so that no oil seeps in.

8. Heat the wok and add oil for deep-frying. When the oil is
   ready, slide the packages in, about 6 at a time so as not to
   overcrowd the wok. Cook for about 3 minutes. Drain on
   paper towels. Alternatively, bake the packets at 350ºF for
   20–30 minutes.

Chef's Hint: After 20 minutes in the oven, open a packet to see if the chicken
is cooked but not dry.

> MARCO POLO recorded that Kublai Khan celebrated Jewish,
> Muslim and Christian ceremonies, because there were enough adher-
> ents of these faiths to merit this kind of attention.

TEA EGGS

12 servings

These eggs look like marbles and taste of anise and spice.

12 eggs
2 tablespoons kosher salt
3 tablespoons black tea
3 tablespoons soy sauce
½ teaspoon sugar
2 whole star anise

1. Place the eggs in a pot with cold water and bring to a boil. Lower the heat and cook, covered, for 5 minutes.
2. Turn off the heat and let stand for 20 minutes. Pour out the water and gently crack shells all over.
3. Return the eggs to the pot and add water to just cover. Add the remaining ingredients, stir once and bring to a boil.
4. Turn heat as low as possible and cook for 2–3 hours. Turn off heat and let the eggs sit in liquid overnight.
5. Peel shells, cut eggs into quarters and arrange on platter to show the fine patterns. The eggs can be stored *unpeeled* for two weeks in the refrigerator.

FISH TOAST

~30 pieces

Shrimp toast is a popular and tasty Chinese appetizer. The fish paste is the same one I use when I make mock shrimp for mock shrimp dishes.

FISH PASTE:

¾ pound white fish fillets, such
  as snapper, sea bass or tilapia
  (don't use cod or haddock)
1 tablespoon minced scallion
1 teaspoon Asian sesame oil
2 tablespoons minced water chestnuts
1 tablespoon sherry
1 teaspoon salt
⅛ teaspoon white pepper
2 teaspoons cornstarch
1 egg white
3 tablespoons water
commercial white bread,
  with crusts removed
several sprigs coriander

1. Cut the fish into 1-inch pieces and chop with the remaining ingredients (except the bread) just until the mixture holds together.
2. Using a cookie or biscuit cutter or a small glass, cut bread circles of about 2 inches in diameters.
3. Spread the fish paste on each round, mounding it in the middle a bit. Place one coriander leaf in the middle.
4. Heat oil until hot and then fry the fish toasts fish side down first, until golden brown, turning once or twice during frying. Drain.

SWEET AND SOUR DAIKON RADISH   4–5 servings

Many of the better Chinese restaurants serve this crunchy snack instead of the ubiquitous fried noodles with duck sauce.

> 1 medium-sized daikon Chinese radish
>   (found in many supermarkets)
>   or ½ pound red radishes
> 1 tablespoon salt
> 1 tablespoon soy sauce
> 2 tablespoons white distilled
>   or rice wine vinegar
> 2 tablespoons sugar
> 1½ tablespoons Asian sesame oil

1. Trim off the ends of the radish, and peel (if using daikon).
2. Slice ¼-inch thick.
3. Salt the radish slices and let marinate for 30 minutes.
4. Rinse off and add the remaining ingredients. Marinate for several hours in the refrigerator.

Chef's Hint: Add some small pieces of bok choy or Chinese broccoli for color.

THE JEWISH Cemetery of Harbin has over 500 Jewish graves.

HOT SPICY CABBAGE

This is a Chinese version of the Korean "kimchee."

1 teaspoon white peppercorns
2–4 hot red peppers, seeded
1 pound napa or bok choy,
   cut into 2-inch pieces
½ tablespoon salt
2½ tablespoons rice wine vinegar
1 tablespoon soy sauce
1–2 bell peppers, finely sliced
10 very thin slices fresh ginger,
   crushed with the side of a knife
⅛ cup each sesame and vegetable oil

1. Stir-fry the peppercorns and red peppers in very hot oil for 10 seconds.
2. Remove from heat and add to the remaining ingredients; mix thoroughly, and chill in tightly covered container for 3–4 hours. This dish improves in the refrigerator with time.

CANDIED PECANS OR WALNUTS

These can be served as a garnish or used in meat dishes or put into little bowls and served as an appetizer with plum wine at the beginning of a Chinese meal.

> ½ pound pecans or walnuts
> 1 cup white sugar

1. Mix the sugar and nuts.
2. Put the mixture into a frying pan or wok and stir until the sugar caramelizes. Watch carefully, as the sugar goes quickly from caramelizing to burning.
3. Pour onto sheets of lightly oiled wax paper.

Chef's Hint: These nuts will disappear very quickly, so make a lot of them.

INSCRIPTIONS ON a Kaifeng steele (stone) discovered in 1489 say that the first synogogue there was built in 1163, and the Jews were ordered by the emperor to follow their faith and settle in Kaifeng. There are stone inscriptions from 1489, 1512, 1663 and 1674 which celebrate repairs of the synagogue through the centuries.

面

NOODLES AND RICE

Chinese cuisine has outstanding dishes using rice and wheat noodles of many varieties. My own children love noodle dishes more than any other Chinese food.

You can find Chinese noodles, fresh, frozen and dried, in almost any Chinese grocery.

For dried rice noodles, use medium width ones (⅜-inch). Frozen wheat noodles can be found in some supermarkets (lo mein noodles). Italian linguine or spaghetti works fine, producing very tasty dishes, but without the exact texture that authentic Chinese noodles have.

One special type of rice noodle is cellophane noodles, which are very thin and sold in nest shapes.

I include a terrific fried rice recipe for the kids.

ANTS CLIMBING A TREE

4–6 servings

This is a terrific dish. The "ants" are bits of meat or vegetarian gluten served in iceberg lettuce leaves and eaten like a taco.

MARINADE:

2 tablespoons soy sauce

2 teaspoons cornstarch

1 tablespoon water

1 tablespoon vegetable oil

1 teaspoon Asian sesame oil

1 tablespoon minced fresh ginger

½ pound lean ground beef or
   diced vegetarian gluten, diced

½ cup finely diced water chestnuts

½ red bell pepper, finely diced

¼ cup finely diced bamboo shoots

6 dried shiitake mushrooms,
   soaked for 30 minutes, squeezed
   and then finely diced

1 cup chicken stock

1 tablespoon sherry

1 tablespoon soy sauce

1 tablespoon cornstarch mixed
   with 2 tablespoons water

½ teaspoon chili pepper flakes
   or hot chili oil to taste

¼ pound thin rice stick noodles
   or cellophane noodles

oil for deep-frying

1. Marinate the ground meat or gluten in the marinade ingredients and let sit for 15 minutes.
2. Stir-fry the meat in a few tablespoons of oil until it is no longer pink.
3. Add the vegetables and stir-fry for 1–2 minutes.
4. Add the stock, sherry, soy sauce, cornstarch mixture and chili and heat until thickened. Remove and set aside.
5. Heat the oil in wok or pot until it is almost smoking and a scallion spins wildly when placed in it. Add the rice stick noodles and stir for 1–2 minutes, stirring constantly, until the noodles puff up.
6. Remove the cooked noodles and toss with the meat mixture.

Chef's Hint: The noodles are said to resemble tree bark and the tiny pieces of meat and vegetables resemble ants.

KAIFENG JEWS prayed facing westward towards Jerusalem and wore blue head coverings to distinguish themselves from Muslims, who wore white head coverings.

LO MEIN WITH PEANUT SAUCE   4–6 servings

This dish is a winner, particularly with small children. It is part of many of my family banquet menus.

> 12 ounces fresh Chinese lo mein
>   noodles or thick spaghetti
> 4 tablespoons Asian sesame oil
> 8 scallions, chopped
> 5 cloves garlic, minced
> 1 tablespoon peeled and
>   minced fresh ginger
> ¼–½ cup honey or brown sugar
> ¼–½ cup creamy peanut butter
> ¼ cup soy sauce
> ¼ cup water
> ¼ cup white distilled or
>   rice wine vinegar
> 1½ tablespoons chili-garlic sauce or
>   ¼ teaspoon red pepper flakes to taste
> 2 cups mung bean sprouts
> 1 cup julienned cucumbers
> 1 cup finely shredded carrots

1. Cook the noodles in boiling water until al dente, cooked enough to be firm, but not soft, and rinse several times until the water is clear.
2. Transfer pasta to a large bowl and add 3 tablespoons of Asian sesame oil. Toss to coat.
3. Heat the remaining 1 tablespoon of oil in a large, heavy skillet over medium–high heat.

4. Add ¾ of the scallions and all of the garlic and ginger. Sauté for about 2 minutes.

5. Add honey or brown sugar, peanut butter, soy sauce, water, vinegar and chili-garlic sauce; whisk to blend until the sauce has the consistency of light cream.

6. Simmer the sauce for 1 minute. Cool to room temperature. Pour over the pasta and toss to coat.

7. Add ¾ of the sprouts, cucumbers and carrots. Mix well. Transfer to the platter and sprinkle with the remaining vegetables for a nice presentation. Serve immediately.

Chef's Hint: This sauce, like all sauces, needs to be prepared to taste because of the saltiness of the different soy sauce brands and pungency of the vinegars used. I like my peanut sauces a bit sweeter than some. Others like them hotter than I do. Using orange juice instead of water makes the dish even more interesting.

CHOW FUN

4–6 servings

My Chinese friend and chef, Simon Teng, told me that if you are in an unfamiliar Chinese restaurant and don't know what to order, order chow fun. This chow fun version is for beef. Most Chinese restaurants offer vegetarian, chicken and seafood versions as well.

10 ounces chow fun noodles (flat rice
    noodles) or wide wheat egg noodles
1 pound beef flank steak, thinly sliced

MARINADE FOR THE MEAT:
    ¼ teaspoon baking soda
    1 tablespoon soy sauce
    1 tablespoon cornstarch
    1 egg white
    1 tablespoon oil

OTHER INGREDIENTS:
    7 tablespoons oil
    2 cloves garlic, finely chopped
    1 slice fresh ginger, julienned
    1 tablespoon sherry
    ½ yellow onion, peeled
      and sliced vertically
    ½ sweet green bell pepper,
      cored and julienned
    1 cup fresh bean sprouts
    ¼ cup chopped cilantro leaves

SAUCE:
    1 tablespoon soy sauce

¼ teaspoon sugar
1 tablespoon sherry
¼ teaspoon white pepper
1 tablespoon vegetarian oyster
    sauce or mushroom sauce

---

1. Cook the noodles in boiling water until al dente, cooked enough to be firm, but not soft, and rinse several times until the water is clear.
2. Slice the meat and mix with the marinade. Let marinate for 15 minutes.
3. Heat 2 tablespoons of oil in the wok until hot.
4. Toss the noodles in the oil until they are very hot and begin to color just a bit on the edges. Remove and set aside.
5. Heat 3 tablespoons of oil in the wok and stir-fry the garlic and ginger for 30 seconds.
6. Add the sherry, onion and green pepper and stir-fry for 1 more minute.
7. Remove and set aside.
8. Heat 2 tablespoons of oil in the wok a final time and add the meat.
9. Stir-fry only until the meat begins to brown.
10. Return the vegetables, noodles and sauce to the wok and toss with the meat until hot.
11. Add the bean sprouts. Toss just a minute or so and sprinkle with the coriander.

Chef's Hint: I fear that many cooks will look at all the ingredients and sequential steps in the recipe above and say, "No way!" Remember, though, if you organize it all beforehand, it really moves quickly. You can substitute chicken or tofu for the meat.

CHOW MEIN   4–6 servings

Chow mein is a staple in Chinese-American restaurants. This is a version unlike the goop you get in many poor-quality Chinese restaurants. It takes a while to assemble all the ingredients; but it is worth the effort. The origin of the name of this dish is interesting. "Chow" is an Americanization of the word "Chao," meaning stir-fry. "Mein" means noodles. The fried noodles normally served at Chinese-American restaurants are not authentic, although tasty. This version is more authentic.

½ pound dried or fresh egg
  noodles or flat rice noodles
3 cloves garlic, crushed
2 teaspoons finely chopped fresh ginger
¼ cup sliced bamboo shoots
½ pound mushrooms, cut into quarters
1 stalk celery, sliced thin diagonally
2 tablespoons vegetable oil
3 scallions, sliced on diagonal
2 tablespoons soy sauce
3 tablespoons vegetable
  or chicken stock
1 tablespoon dry sherry
1 teaspoon sugar
¼ pound bean sprouts
½ pound chicken or beef or
  firm tofu, thinly sliced
1 tablespoon cornstarch
  mixed with ¼ cup water
2 tablespoons chopped cilantro, leaves

1. Cook the noodles until al dente, cooked enough to be firm, but not soft, and rinse with cold water several times.
2. Stir-fry the garlic and ginger in 1 tablespoon of very hot oil and then add meat (optional). Stir-fry until it loses its color. Remove.
3. Add bamboo shoots and mushrooms and stir-fry for 1 minute.
4. Add the remaining ingredients with meat (optional) and simmer for 2 minutes until thickened.
5. Pour the vegetable/meat mixture over the noodles and serve with cilantro on top as garnish.

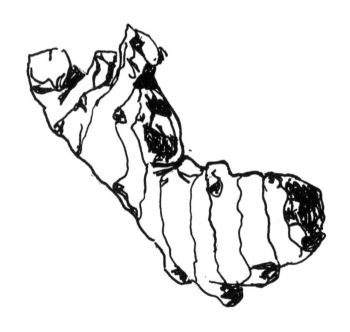

NOODLES IN BROWN SAUCE   4–6 servings

This recipe is modified from one published by Millie Chan. Brown sauce is a master sauce often found in Chinese dishes.

1 pound lo mein or egg noodles
4 tablespoons vegetable oil
1 tablespoon Asian sesame oil
2 cloves garlic, minced
1 pound ground turkey,
    veal, beef or gluten
1 tablespoon sherry
½ cup vegetable or chicken broth
2 teaspoons sugar
3 tablespoons soy sauce
4 tablespoons hoisin sauce
2 teaspoons cornstarch mixed
    with 4 teaspoons water
1 cucumber, peeled and seeded,
    then julienned or shredded
¼ cup chopped scallions
salt to taste

1. Cook the noodles until al dente, cooked till firm, but not soft. Rinse with cold water several times and reserve.
2. Heat the vegetable and Asian sesame oils in wok and add garlic. Stir-fry for 15 seconds.
3. Add the meat and stir-fry until no longer pink.
4. Add sherry, broth, sugar and the soy and hoisin sauces. Stir and heat until simmering. Add the cornstarch mixture until sauce thickens.
5. Mix the meat mixture with noodles and top with cucumber and scallions.

SZECHWAN NOODLES

4–6 servings

This is Chinese comfort food, served on the streets.

1 pound fresh lo mein or
  ¾ pound dried egg noodles
½ pound ground beef, veal or chicken
3 tablespoons soy sauce
2 tablespoons dry sherry
¼ teaspoon ground white pepper
2 tablespoons vegetarian oyster
  or mushroom sauce
2 tablespoons peanut butter
1 tablespoon white distilled
  or rice wine vinegar
1 cup chicken broth
5 tablespoons Asian sesame oil
1 tablespoon fresh minced ginger
6 cloves garlic, minced
¾ teaspoon hot pepper flakes
2 scallions, thinly sliced
2 cups bean sprouts
Szechwan pepper to taste,
  ground (if available)

1. Cook noodles until al dente, cooked enough to be firm, but not soft. Rinse with cold water several times and reserve.

2. Combine the meat with 1 tablespoon of soy sauce, sherry and ¼ teaspoon of ground white pepper. Let marinate for 30 minutes.

3. Combine the mushroom or vegetarian oyster sauce with the remaining 2 tablespoons of soy sauce, peanut butter, vinegar and chicken stock, whisking smooth.

4. Heat 4 tablespoons of sesame oil and cook the meat until it loses its pinkness. Stir in the ginger, garlic and red pepper flakes and cook until fragrant.

5. Add the sauce mixture and remaining tablespoon of sesame oil.

6. Heat noodles with hot water, drain and then pour sauce over them.

7. Sprinkle with scallions, bean sprouts and Szechwan ground pepper.

MATTEO RICCI, an Italian Jesuit missionary, discovered Kaifeng's synagogue in the 17th century.

FRIED RICE

4–6 servings

Fried rice is made with cold cooked rice. You can add almost anything to the rice in this dish, leftover meats and vegetables. It is the perfect meal for a Sunday dinner if you want to finish off the Shabbat roast chicken.

4 cups cold cooked rice
4 tablespoons vegetable oil
1 tablespoon Asian sesame oil
1 teaspoon chopped garlic
¼ cup chopped scallions
2 teaspoons chopped fresh ginger
1 cup finely diced cooked
 or raw beef or chicken
½ cup chopped celery
2 eggs, beaten
1 tablespoon kosher salt to taste
2 tablespoons soy sauce
½–¾ cup frozen peas or pea pods
½ cup bean sprouts or chopped lettuce

1. Separate the rice with your hands.
2. Mix the oils and put one half in the wok and heat until very hot.
3. Add the garlic, scallions and ginger, and stir-fry for 15 seconds.
4. Add the meat and celery and stir-fry until celery is just cooked. Remove from the wok.
5. Heat remaining oil in the wok and add the rice. Cook until well heated for about 5 minutes.

6. Spread the rice to the edges of the wok and in the middle;
    add the eggs and let them cook, scrambling them during
    the process.
7. Mix the eggs with the rice and then add the remaining
    ingredients. Mix and cook until hot.

Chef's Hint: You can't use too much ginger and garlic. Feel free to double
the amounts. After I mix the eggs with the rice, I like to let the rice sit in
the hot wok long enough to form a crust. A metal spatula can be used to
scrape this succulent toasty-tasting crust into the mass of rice before adding the vegetables.

素食

VEGETARIAN

The Chinese have a long tradition of outstanding vegetarian foods. I offer complete vegetarian dinners at banquets for those who don't eat meat. There are many soy products that mimic meat and seafood and are used at Chinese vegetarian restaurants. Many of these ingredients are hard to find other than in major cities. Some are fairly hard to work with unless you have some hands-on training. My selection of Chinese vegetarian recipes can be easily made from common ingredients found in American markets.

BROCCOLI SALAD
4–6 servings

This is a simple salad that presents a bright green side dish with meat dishes or a nice vegetarian entrée in a larger meal.

1 bunch broccoli, separated into florets
1 teaspoon kosher salt
3 tablespoons sesame seeds

DRESSING:
3 tablespoons soy sauce
1 tablespoon white vinegar
1 teaspoon sugar
2 teaspoons Asian sesame oil

1. Steam or parboil the florets until bright green. Drain in a colander, and then chill quickly in cold water or ice water.
2. Place the sesame seeds and salt in a dry heated frying pan and stir, toasting them until the seeds turn light brown.
3. Mix the dressing and broccoli and sprinkle on the sesame seeds.

COLD SWEET AND SOUR CHINESE CABBAGE

6 servings

This is an easy vegetable dish that is popular with everyone.

2 pounds white Chinese cabbage (napa)
2 teaspoons kosher salt
7 tablespoons sugar
⅓ cup white distilled vinegar
1 fresh red chili pepper, finely shredded

1. Cut the napa leaves crosswise into 2-inch pieces and then julienne. There will be about 8 cups of cabbage.
2. Salt the cabbage and let sit for 1 hour.
3. Put the cabbage in a dishtowel and squeeze out as much water as you can. Reserve the liquid in a bowl.
4. Heat the sugar and vinegar until boiling, and pour over the cabbage. Let sit for 30 minutes.
5. Strain the liquid from the cabbage using a colander; reserve and boil a second time and pour it again over the cabbage.
6. Cover and refrigerate for 2–3 days or up to a week. When serving, remove the cabbage from the liquid, add red chili pepper and toss.

VEGETABLE MU SHU

4–6 servings

This is a vegetarian version of mu shu meat dishes, served in wheat pancakes. You can sometimes buy the pancakes in Asian markets. If you do not wish to make them from scratch, you can substitute thin flour tortillas, as suggested in the Chef's Hint at the end.

> 10 large Chinese black mushrooms, softened
> several wood ears (fungus), softened (optional)
> 1 pound extra firm tofu
> ½ pound pea pods or napa cabbage
> 2 carrots, cut on the diagonal
> 2 scallions, cut on the diagonal
> 2 ounces cellophane noodles,
>   soaked until soft
> 1 teaspoon vegetable oil
> hoisin sauce
> Mandarin pancakes

SEASONING
> ½ teaspoon kosher salt
> ½ teaspoon sugar
> 2 tablespoons soy sauce
> ¼ cup water
> 2 scant teaspoons Asian sesame oil

1. Julienne the mushrooms, tofu and vegetables.
2. Cut the noodles into 2-inch pieces.
3. Stir-fry the vegetables and tofu for 15 seconds in oil, and add the rest of the ingredients.
4. Simmer until the moisture from the vegetables has evaporated. Serve with mandarin pancakes (see following recipe) and hoisin sauce.

MANDARIN PANCAKES

2–3 cups flour
1 cup warm water
½ teaspoon salt
oil

1. Mix the flour, water and salt and knead until it forms a ball of medium soft dough.
2. Lightly oil the dough and let rest in a bowl for 15 minutes.
3. Roll the dough into a rope and cut it cross-wise into an even number of 2-inch long pieces.
4. Roll each piece into a ball and flatten it with your palm into a 2–3-inch wide disk.
5. Heavily oil one side of a dough disk and place it, oiled side down, onto a non-oiled dough disk, making a "dough-oil sandwich."
6. Flour the top and bottom of the sandwich and roll it into a 5–6 inch wide flour pancake, about ⅛ inch thick. Repeat until all the dough is used up.
7. Heat a non-stick frying pan or wok until very hot. Do not add oil to the pan.
8. Place a flour pancake in the pan. It will puff up as the oil bubbles between the dough.
9. Quickly turn the pancake over for 10 seconds and then remove it from the heat.
10. Finally, carefully pull apart the two very thin pancakes.

Chef's Hint: Homemade Mandarin pancakes are great. However, you can also buy commercial versions in some Asian markets as "mu shu wrappers." In a pinch, you can substitute the thinnest flour tortilla or wheat wrap you can find, cutting it into 6x6-inch pieces.

SZECHWAN SPICY EGGPLANT
4–6 servings

Eggplant made Asian style is simply heaven to me – a must in almost any of my Chinese dinners. This recipe is a favorite at my large dinners.

> 1 small Chinese eggplant
>   (about ¾ pound)
> 6 tablespoons vegetable oil
> 2 tablespoons chopped cilantro leaves

SAUCE:

> 1 tablespoon vegetable oil
> 1 tablespoon finely minced fresh ginger
> 1 clove garlic, finely minced
> 2 tablespoons hot chili flakes or to taste
> 2 tablespoons water
> 1 tablespoon soy sauce
> ½ teaspoon sugar
> ½ teaspoon kosher salt

1. Cut off and discard the eggplant stem. Cut the Chinese eggplant, skin and all, into 1-inch cubes. (Black Beauty eggplants, the variety normally found in supermarkets, must be peeled first.)
2. Soak the eggplant in cold water for 10 minutes to keep it from absorbing too much oil when fried.
3. Drain the eggplant and blot with paper towels to remove surface water.
4. Heat oil until very hot in a wok or frying pan and sauté the eggplant for about 5 minutes.
5. Add ¼ cup of water; cover and braise until done, about 5–10 minutes.
6. Remove with a slotted spoon and drain on paper towels.

SAUCE:

1. Heat 1 tablespoon of oil until very hot.
2. Add the ginger and garlic and stir-fry for a few seconds.
3. Add the remaining sauce ingredients; stir and bring to a boil.
4. Pour the sauce over the eggplant and garnish with cilantro. Serve hot or cold.

Chef's Hint: Use Asian eggplants, which are never bitter – they look like bananas. You don't have to peel them, either.

THE CHINESE referred to the Jews as those "who pull the sinews", in reference to the butchering skills needed to make meat kosher.

STIR-FRIED SPINACH OR OTHER GREENS

4–6 servings

This is a generic recipe that is good for spinach, Chinese broccoli, bok choy and pea pod greens.

1 teaspoon Asian sesame oil
2 cloves garlic, chopped
3 thin slices fresh ginger
1 pound greens, cut into small pieces
½ cup water or chicken stock
pinch sugar
¼ teaspoon salt
1–2 tablespoons cornstarch mixed
   with 2–4 tablespoons water

1. Heat oil in a wok and add garlic and ginger, stir-frying until soft, for about 30 seconds.
2. Add the greens and stir-fry to coat.
3. Add water or stock, sugar and salt, and stir-fry until greens are just done and bright green, about 1–2 minutes.
4. Slowly add the cornstarch mixture to thicken the sauce as desired.

TOFU AND MUSHROOMS IN VINEGAR SAUCE

4–6 servings

If you like mushrooms, you will like this.

1 teaspoon minced garlic

1 tablespoon oil

5 dried shiitake mushrooms, soaked,
squeezed dry and sliced

5 oyster mushrooms, sliced

1 pound soft tofu, cut into 1-inch cubes

3 scallions, sliced diagonally

½ cup chicken broth or
vegetarian substitute

SAUCE:

2 tablespoons rice wine vinegar

1 tablespoon soy sauce

1 tablespoon sugar

½ teaspoon chili flakes

½ tablespoon cornstarch

1. Stir-fry the garlic in oil.
2. Add the mushrooms and tofu and stir-fry for 2 minutes
   or until the mushrooms are cooked.
3. Add the scallions and cook for 15 seconds.
4. Add the broth and sauce and cook until slightly
   thickened.

MAPO TOFU

4–6 servings

This hot and spicy tofu dish is a favorite with people who like hot and spicy food. You can substitute ground beef, turkey, veal or chicken if you want a meat version.

    1½ pounds medium-firm to firm tofu
    3 tablespoons vegetable oil
    ¼ pound ground vegetarian protein
    ¼ teaspoon salt
    1 teaspoon fermented black beans
    1 tablespoon chopped garlic
    1 teaspoon chili paste or
       chili flakes to taste
    1 leek or 3 scallions
    3 tablespoons vegetarian
       or chicken stock
    1 scallion, sliced in thin, slanted pieces

SAUCE MIXTURE:
    1 tablespoon cornstarch
    2 tablespoons water
    2 tablespoons soy sauce
    1 teaspoon Asian sesame oil

1. Cut the tofu into ¼-inch-square cubes and put them into boiling water for 2 minutes; remove and drain.
2. Chop the leek or scallions into short diagonal pieces.
3. Heat oil in a wok and fry the vegetable protein for 1 minute.
4. Add salt, fermented black beans, garlic, chili paste or flakes, tofu, scallions or leek, and stock.

5. Turn down the heat. Cook for 3–4 minutes. Add the
    sauce mixture and cook until thickened.
6. Sprinkle the sliced single scallion on top and serve.

Chef's Hint: This dish gets hotter the longer it sticks around. If you make it
one day and then serve it the next, it will be even better.

DEEP-FRIED CHINESE GREENS   4–6 servings

This is a crunchy, almost confetti-like, vegetarian side dish, garnish or mixture for meat dishes. It is fun to make.

> 1 pound bok choy leaves (green part),
>   Chinese broccoli leaves
>   or large spinach leaves
> oil for deep-frying
> ½ teaspoon sugar
> ¼ teaspoon salt to taste

1. Roll up the leaves into cigar-like tight rolls and then slice them across as finely as you can to make very thin strips.
2. Heat the oil until very hot and in batches, cook the vegetable until it shrivels and becomes crispy, for about 15 seconds. Remove and drain on paper towel.
3. Toss with sugar and salt.

Chef's Hint: Hide this dish or it will disappear, melting in the mouths of family and guests.

DOUBLE COOKED STRING BEANS 4–6 servings

These are very good served in mu shu pancakes with hoisin sauce.

 2 cups vegetable oil
 3–6 cloves garlic, diced
 1 pound string beans
 1–2 tablespoons soy sauce or to taste

1. Heat 2 tablespoons of oil until very hot and then stir-fry the garlic until it just turns light brown and remove. Add the rest of the oil and heat.
2. Add beans and deep-fry for 1–2 minutes until they shrivel. Remove. Drain all but a few tablespoons of oil.
3. Re-heat oil in a wok until hot. Add beans and garlic and stir-fry for 1 minute. Add soy sauce; stir to mix and serve.

FISH

Chinese cooking has a marvelous fish and seafood cuisine. Even though Jews following kashrut can't eat shellfish, there is still a wide variety of mock classic seafood dishes to prepare, along with terrific fish.

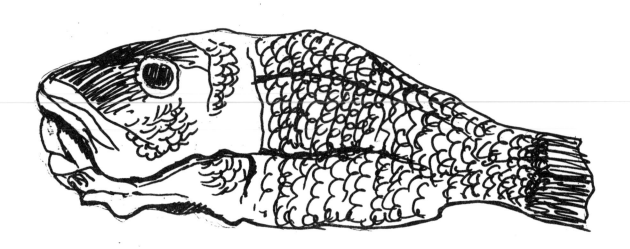

STEAMED FISH WITH GINGER AND SCALLIONS

4–6 servings

This simple, fresh-tasting, fish dish is one of my most requested items at my Chinese dinners and banquets. One time, I invited an undergraduate Chinese exchange student for lunch at China Road Restaurant. She said she despaired of ever getting good Chinese food in America. I told her she could order anything from the menu, and she ordered Steamed Fish with Ginger and Scallions. It was what her grandmother made back in Malaysia.

1–2 pounds whole fish or fish fillets
2 tablespoons sherry
½ teaspoon kosher salt

SAUCE:
1 tablespoon Asian sesame oil
2 tablespoons vegetable oil
¼ cup finely shredded fresh ginger
¼ cup finely shredded scallions
3 tablespoons soy sauce
2 tablespoons white distilled
   or rice wine vinegar
½ teaspoon sugar
chopped cilantro leaves, for garnish

1. Smear the fish with sherry and salt, and let sit for 5 minutes.
2. Place the fish on a serving plate and place in a wok. Steam until done for 7–12 minutes.
3. While fish is steaming, heat oils until they are very hot, and stir-fry the ginger for 15 seconds. Add the scallions; stir-fry for 5 seconds and turn off heat.

4. Add soy sauce, vinegar and sugar and stir until the sugar dissolves. Keep hot until the fish is ready.
5. Top the fish with the sauce, and then the cilantro.

Chef's Hint: You can put the fish in aluminum foil and bake it for 10 minutes at 350°F, and sauce it after; or you can cook the fish at high heat with ½ cup of water, covered, in a microwave oven for about 7 minutes or until it flakes.

SALT AND PEPPER FISH STRIPS
4–6 servings

This recipe is a modification of the famous Chinese dish, Salt and Pepper Shrimp, which involves taking peeled shrimp, dusting them with cornstarch, deep-frying them and then serving them with a spicy salt and pepper sauce. I've made the dish kosher by using perch or red snapper fillets.

¾ pound red snapper or perch
   fillets (don't use cod or haddock),
   sliced into ½ x 2-inch pieces
2 teaspoons cornstarch mixed
   with 1 tablespoon sherry
2 cups oil for deep-frying
1 teaspoon Asian sesame oil
1 teaspoon chopped garlic
1 teaspoon chopped fresh ginger
1 teaspoon coarse salt
⅛ teaspoon white pepper
1 tablespoon minced scallion
½ head iceberg lettuce, thinly sliced

1. Marinate the sliced fish in sherry and cornstarch for 15 minutes. Put oil in a wok and heat until a scallion sizzles when dropped in. Deep-fry the fish in oil until golden. Remove the fish.
2. Remove the oil except for 1 tablespoons. Add sesame oil and stir-fry the garlic, ginger, salt and pepper for 30 seconds and add fish for 1 minute. Add the scallion and the remove everything from the pan.
3. Stir-fry the lettuce in a heated pan with 1 tablespoon of remaining oil until slightly limp. Put the fish on the lettuce and serve.

STIR FRIED FISH STRIPS WITH ASPARAGUS

4–6 servings

This is another dish that originally was conceived for shrimp, but works well with fish strips.

¾ pound red snapper or perch
  fillets (don't use cod or haddock),
  sliced into ½ x 2-inch pieces
2 teaspoons cornstarch mixed
  with 1 tablespoon sherry
2 slices fresh ginger
2 tablespoons vegetable oil
1 pound asparagus, sliced in
  1-inch pieces on the diagonal
2 tablespoons soy sauce
1 tablespoon sherry
1 teaspoon sugar

1. Marinate the sliced fish in sherry and cornstarch for 15 minutes. Deep-fry in oil until golden. Set aside.
2. Stir-fry the ginger in oil until the ginger turns brown.
3. Add the asparagus, soy sauce, sherry and sugar. Cook, covered for 2 minutes.
4. Add the fish; mix and serve.

ASIAN FISH IN PACKETS
4 servings

This is modified from a recipe from the *Moosewood Restaurant Cooks at Home*, by The Moosewood Collective, Simon and Schuster, 1994. It is an easy way to make a "mock" steamed fish very delicious.

4 4–6 ounce fish fillets
1 cup cooked cold rice
2 cups bok choy, coarsely chopped
4 scallions, chopped
1 tablespoon vegetable oil
1 teaspoon grated fresh ginger
1 clove garlic, minced
2 tablespoons soy sauce
2 tablespoons Asian sesame oil
chili oil (optional)

1. Preheat the oven to 450ºF.
2. Take four 12 x 24-inch sheets of aluminum foil. Fold each over to make a double-thick square and brush a little vegetable oil in the center of each square.
3. Rinse the fish in water.
4. Spread ¼ of the rice on the center of each foil square and then layer the greens, fish and scallions on top of the rice.
5. In a small bowl, combine the vegetable oil, ginger, garlic, soy sauce, Asian sesame oil and a few drops of optional chili oil. Pour ¼ of the sauce over each serving. Fold the foil into airtight packets. Place pockets on a baking sheet. Bake for 20 minutes.
6. Open a packet and check that the fish is cooked and serve or transfer the contents onto plates.

BRAISED HOT AND SOUR FISH   4–6 servings

This is a delicious, spicy dish.

    1–2 pounds bluefish or salmon fillets

MARINADE:
    2 tablespoons white wine
    ½ teaspoon white pepper
    cornstarch
    2 cups and 1 tablespoon oil
    1 tablespoon minced garlic
    pinch salt
    2 cups chicken broth
    1 teaspoon–1 tablespoon hot
      pepper flakes (to taste)
    1 tablespoon minced fresh ginger
    2–3 tablespoons soy sauce
    2 tablespoons white distilled vinegar
    2 scallions, cut into 1-inch pieces
    1 tablespoon cornstarch mixed
      with 2 tablespoons water
    1 teaspoon Asian sesame oil

1. Slice the fillets to the skin, but not through it, in a 2-inch checkerboard pattern.
2. Marinate the fish in wine and white pepper for 5–10 minutes.
3. Roll the fish in cornstarch. Heat the oil in a wok until smoking hot and fry fish on both sides until golden brown. Set aside.

4. Clean the wok and add 1 tablespoon of oil. Heat until smoking hot.
5. Add garlic and salt, mashing together. Stir-fry for 10 seconds.
6. Add the fish to a wok. Pour in the chicken broth and bring to a boil.
7. Add hot pepper, ginger and soy sauce. Reduce heat and simmer for 5 minutes, turning fish.
8. Add vinegar and scallions to sauce.
9. Remove the fish. Add the cornstarch mixture and Asian sesame oil and stir until sauce thickens. Pour over the fish.

RED COOKED WHOLE FISH

4–6 servings

"Red cooking" refers to the soy sauce in the cooking liquid, which adds color and flavor to meat or fish. Whole bass, tilapia, trout or carp are excellent choices.

> 4 dried black mushrooms, softened
>   in hot water for 30 minutes
> 1 whole fish, about 1 ½ pounds,
>   cleaned, with head and tail on
> 1 tablespoon cornstarch
> 4 tablespoons vegetable oil
> 2 slices fresh gingerroot, minced
> 2 cloves garlic, minced
> 2 scallions, cut into 2-inch lengths
> 2 tablespoons rice wine vinegar
> 4 tablespoons soy sauce
> ½ teaspoon sugar
> ½ cup shredded bamboo shoots
> ¾ cup water
> cilantro leaves, for garnish

1. Shred the mushrooms and set aside.
2. Rinse the fish and dry with a paper towel. Slice fish on both sides in a 2-inch checkerboard pattern, not cutting through the bone. Dust with cornstarch.
3. Heat the oil until almost smoking in a wok and fry the fish about 2 minutes on both sides.
4. Add the ginger, garlic and scallions and continue to fry the fish for another 2 minutes, until lightly browned.
5. Sprinkle on the vinegar and cover the wok for 30 seconds.
6. Uncover and add the soy sauce, sugar, mushrooms,

bamboo shoots and water. Cover the pan and simmer over medium heat for about 5 minutes, frequently basting the fish with the sauce. There should be about ½ cup of sauce at the end.

7. Transfer the fish to a large oblong serving platter and pour the sauce with the mushrooms and bamboo shoots over the fish. Serve immediately with cilantro leaves as garnish.

SWEET AND SOUR FRIED FISH   4–6 servings

This fish dish is deep-fried and served with a familiar Chinese sweet and sour sauce. In some sense, this dish is Chinese-American in taste and texture. The version here is modified from Millie Chan's cookbook.

> 1 pound sole, flounder or scrod
>   fillets, cut into 2-inch pieces

MARINADE:
> ½ teaspoon kosher salt
> 1 teaspoon soy sauce
> 1 teaspoon Asian sesame oil
> ⅛ teaspoon white pepper
> 1 teaspoon sherry

BATTER:
> ½ cup all-purpose flour
> ¼ cup cornstarch
> 2 teaspoons baking powder
> ½ teaspoon kosher salt
> ⅔ cup cold water
> 1 tablespoon oil
>
> 2 cups vegetable oil

SWEET AND SOUR SAUCE:
> 3 tablespoons sugar
> 3 tablespoons white distilled vinegar
> ⅓ cup water
> 1 tablespoon ketchup
> 1 teaspoon soy sauce

2 teaspoons cornstarch
few sprigs fresh coriander, for garnish

---

1. Mix the marinade. Pour over the fish and let sit for 30 minutes.
2. Combine the batter ingredients and stir until smooth.
3. Heat a wok over medium heat until hot; add 2 cups of oil and heat.
4. When the oil is very hot (a piece of scallion will sizzle and "dance" in it), dip the fish pieces into the batter and then into the hot oil.
5. Deep-fry as many pieces as can float freely in the oil until golden brown and crisp for about 2 minutes. Turn each piece several times during frying.
6. Remove and drain; keep warm. Continue the procedure until all the pieces are cooked.
7. Mix the sauce ingredients until there are no cornstarch lumps and heat over medium heat until thickened, stirring constantly until the sauce becomes clear. Serve on the fish with cilantro as garnish.

鸡肉

CHICKEN, DUCK AND OTHER FOWL

There is an infinite number of recipes for chicken, quail and of course, duck, in Chinese cuisine. Duck, in particular, is popular in Chinese kitchens. Unfortunately, duck can be very messy to cook in home kitchens because of the large amount of fat that it renders. For this reason, I seldom make Chinese duck at home or at banquets. Instead, I focus on chicken and also turkey, a very American fowl.

STEAMED CHICKEN WITH SOY SCALLION SAUCE

4–6 servings

This is a very simple dish to make, and delicious as well.

4 chicken breast halves, bone-in
1 tablespoon minced fresh ginger
¼ cup vegetable oil
¼ cup scallions, chopped
    into ¼-inch pieces
2 tablespoons soy sauce
½ teaspoon sugar
1 teaspoon Asian sesame oil

1. Steam the chicken over simmering water for 10–15 minutes until just done. Poaching the chicken in a cup of water is fine too. Make sure you don't overcook it.
2. Stir together the remaining ingredients in a bowl. The mixture should be very salty and strongly flavored.
3. When the chicken is done, cut it into ¼-inch slices and drizzle the sauce on it.

RED COOKED CHICKEN

4–6 servings

The sauce in this dish is wonderful and can be saved frozen for subsequent red cooked dinners. I have read that red cooked sauces in some Chinese households are passed from generation to generation as a culinary legacy, the living record of hundreds of communal family meals. This is a wonderful idea.

1 large chicken, about 3 pounds
3 cups soy sauce
8 cups water
6 tablespoons sherry
8 large slices fresh ginger
2 whole star anise
1 tablespoon orange peel
1 large clove garlic
6 tablespoons sugar
1 cinnamon stick
2 teaspoons Asian sesame oil

1. Rinse the chicken with cold water inside and out and remove the flaps of fat. Put the chicken in a pot, breast down.
2. Boil the remaining ingredients except for the Asian sesame oil in a pot for 20 minutes and add to the chicken. The pot should be large enough so that the chicken is just covered with the sauce.
3. Cover the pot and barely simmer for 15 minutes.
4. Turn the chicken over, replace lid and simmer for another 15 minutes, basting every 5 minutes.
5. Turn off the heat and leave the chicken submerged in liquid in the covered saucepan for 1 hour.

6. Lift chicken out, letting any liquid in the cavity drain back into the saucepan.
7. Brush the chicken all over with Asian sesame oil and chop into large pieces, bones and all.
8. Save the remaining liquid. Refrigerate or freeze and use for red cooking other food. The flavor gets better each time you use it.

THERE IS a street in Kaifeng called, "The Lane of the Sect that Teaches the Scriptures."

KUNG PAO CHICKEN

4–6 servings

This is a popular and spicy chicken dish made with peanuts and chili peppers. According to legend, the dish was made accidentally. A small son of General Tso of the Chin Dynasty tossed some hot peppers as a practical joke into a chicken dish that was being made for his father. Father Tso liked the spice, so the dish was born. General Tso was known as the "Kung Pao," or Guardian of the Heir-Apparent, and the dish was so named.

My version mimics one I once ordered that included diced carrots. The general preparation of the recipe, as well as the story, is modified from the very delicious version offered by Chef Henry Chung at his Hunan Restaurant in San Francisco.

1½ pounds chicken, diced
   into ½-inch cubes
½ tablespoon sherry
1 teaspoon cornstarch
½ cup vegetable oil
4–5 dried hot peppers
3 carrots, peeled and cut
   into ½-inch cubes
1 green or red bell pepper,
   cut into ½-inch cubes
½ tablespoon minced garlic
½ teaspoon minced ginger
½ cup skinless, roasted,
   unsalted peanuts

SAUCE:
   2 tablespoons soy sauce
   1 teaspoon rice wine vinegar
   1 tablespoon minced scallion

½ teaspoon sugar
1 teaspoon Asian sesame oil

1. Marinate the chicken in sherry and cornstarch for
    15 minutes.
2. Heat ¼ cup of the oil in the wok until almost smoking.
    Add the chicken and stir-fry until the meat is no longer
    pink. Remove the chicken. Drain and reserve the oil.
3. Clean the wok if any cornstarch has stuck to it and heat
    remaining oil until smoking hot. Add hot peppers and
    cook until they turn almost black. Add carrots and stir-
    fry for a few minutes until the carrots are almost done.
    Add the bell pepper, garlic and ginger and stir-fry for
    30 seconds to 1 minute more, making sure the garlic does
    not burn.
4. Mix the sauce ingredients and set aside.
5. Stir in the chicken and peanuts, and then add the sauce
    ingredients and stir until well blended.

GENERAL TSO'S CHICKEN   4–6 servings

General Tso not only had Kung Pao Chicken named for him, but this succulent chicken dish as well, made with boned chicken thighs. Chinese cooks
prefer chicken thighs to chicken breasts because thighs have a higher fat
content and do not overcook. In comparison, bland white meat is used in
soup stock or for dipping into pungent sauces.

>   1 large egg, beaten
>   ¼ teaspoon salt
>   ⅛ teaspoon freshly ground
>   white pepper
>   2 tablespoons cornstarch
>   1½ pounds chicken thighs, boned,
>   and cut into 1-inch pieces
>   ½ cup cornstarch for dusting

SAUCE:

>   4 tablespoons soy sauce
>   2 teaspoon minced garlic
>   2 tablespoon minced fresh ginger
>   4 tablespoons hoisin sauce
>   6 teaspoons sugar
>   6 teaspoons white distilled
>   or rice wine vinegar
>   3 teaspoons sherry
>
>   3–4 cups vegetable oil
>   6 small dried hot chili peppers
>   ½ cup finely sliced scallion

1. Mix together the egg, salt and pepper, and 2 tablespoons of cornstarch.
2. Add the chicken cubes; mix to coat, and marinate for 30 minutes. Put ½ cup of cornstarch in a small paper bag and toss in the chicken. Shake to coat the chicken well.
3. Combine the sauce ingredients and set aside.
4. Pour 3 cups of oil into the wok and heat to high (or use a deep-fat fryer).
5. Remove chicken, a handful at a time, and deep-fry for 1½–2 minutes, until the chicken is browned and crisp.
6. Pour off all but 1½ tablespoons of the oil from the wok. Reheat until smoking hot, and add the chilies and stir-fry for 15 seconds.
7. Add the scallion and stir-fry for 30 seconds.
8. Return the chicken and stir-fry for 1 minute. Add sauce ingredients and stir-fry for another 1½ minutes, mixing well.

CHINESE STYLE OVEN-FRIED CHICKEN

4–6 servings

Deep-fat frying pieces of chicken involves a lot of oil. My mother always "oven-fried" her fried chicken, which is equally delicious and not as fattening. Here is a Chinese version, modified from a recipe by Millie Chan. I use Rice Krispies® crumbs and cornstarch to cover the chicken, which gives it an especially crispy exterior.

MARINADE:

1 clove garlic, minced

½ teaspoon fresh ginger, minced

½ teaspoon kosher salt

2 teaspoons sugar

3 tablespoons soy sauce

1 tablespoon sherry

1 frying chicken, about
  3 pounds, cut into 8 pieces

2 tablespoons cornstarch

½ cup Rice Krispies®, ground
  into crumbs, or flour

¼ teaspoon salt

¼ teaspoon five spice powder

3 eggs, beaten with ⅛ cup water

2 tablespoons Asian sesame oil

margarine

1. Combine the marinade ingredients with the chicken and set aside for 1–3 hours.
2. Mix the cornstarch, cereal crumbs, salt and five spice powder.

3. Preheat the oven to 375ºF and coat the pieces of chicken first in egg, and then in crumb mixture or flour.
4. Place chicken pieces on an aluminum-foil-covered baking sheet, coated with Asian sesame oil. The chicken pieces should not touch. Put a ⅛-inch thick pat of margarine on each piece of chicken.
5. Bake for 30–45 minutes until golden brown.

UNCLE TAI'S DICED CHICKEN WITH WALNUTS

4–6 servings

Uncle Tai's was a famous Chinese restaurant in New York City, where stage and movie stars could occasionally be seen. The food was impeccable. One of their signature dishes was Diced Chicken with Walnuts.

1 pound chicken breasts, diced
　　into ¾-inch pieces

MARINADE:
1 egg white
1½ tablespoons sherry
⅛ teaspoon salt
1 tablespoon cornstarch

½ cup vegetable oil
1-inch length fresh ginger, thinly
　　sliced and cut into ⅓-inch pieces
3 ounces walnuts
2 scallions, white part only
　　sliced into pieces
½ teaspoon Asian sesame oil

SAUCE:
2½ tablespoons soy sauce
1½ tablespoons sherry
¾ teaspoon sugar
1 teaspoon cornstarch dissolved
　　in 2 teaspoons water

1. Marinate breasts for up to 2 days in the refrigerator.

2. Heat the oil in a wok until very hot and fry the walnuts until crisp. Set aside.
3. Lower the oil temperature a bit and then stir-fry the chicken until it loses its pinkness and remove.
4. Clean the wok. Add 1 tablespoon of oil and stir-fry the ginger and scallion for a minute. Add chicken, walnuts and sauce and cook until the sauce has thickened. Stir in the Asian sesame oil at the last moment.

Chef's Hint: If you use candied pecans or candied walnuts (see recipe in this book), the dish is even better!

ROCK SUGAR-GINGER CHICKEN
WITH TOFU AND CHESTNUTS   4–6 servings

This is a delicious chicken stew with multiple textures and flavors.

    1 cake medium firm tofu

SAUCE:
    ½ cup chicken broth
    2 tablespoons soy sauce
    2 tablespoons granulated sugar
    ½ cup water

    1 tablespoon vegetable oil
    1 cup thinly sliced fresh ginger
    2 pounds bone-in thighs,
        each cut into 4 pieces
    2 dried shiitake mushrooms,
        soaked, stems removed, cut
        into ½-inch pieces
    3 cloves peeled whole garlic
    ½ can water chestnuts, pieces
        cut into quarters
    1 tablespoon cilantro leaves,
        chopped, for garnish

1. Put the tofu in the freezer overnight. Thaw. The texture will change as the water thaws from the soy protein, giving the tofu a chewy texture. Thaw and squeeze tofu and cut into 1-inch cubes.

2. Heat the chicken broth, soy sauce, sugar and ½ cup of water just to boiling. Reduce the heat to medium low and simmer,

uncovered, until sugar completely dissolves for about
5 minutes.

3. Heat oil in a wok until hot. Add the ginger and cook until
   lightly browned, about 1 minute, stirring constantly.
4. Add chicken thighs, skin-side down, and mushrooms, and
   cook for 4 minutes or until the chicken is browned but not
   cooked through.
5. Add the sauce mixture, garlic, tofu and water chestnuts and
   cook, covered for 5 minutes. Turn the chicken over and cook,
   covered, another 5 minutes or until the juices run clear.
6. Garnish with cilantro.

Chef's Hint: An alternate and more authentic way to get the proper tofu
texture is to slice the tofu into ½-inch slices and deep-fry it until it "shrivels."
Cut it into cubes.

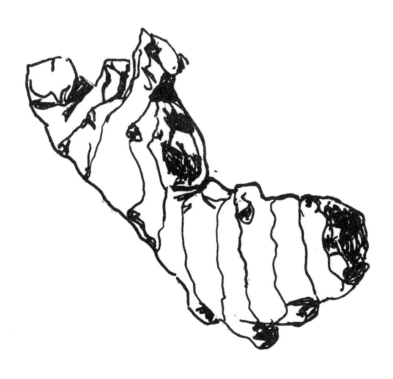

MOO GOO GAI PAN
4–6 servings

Moo Goo Gai Pan, chicken with mushrooms, is a Cantonese Chinese-American dish I remember from my childhood. This version is much better than most found in Chinese-American restaurants.

MARINADE:

1 tablespoon finely grated fresh ginger

1½ teaspoons Asian sesame oil

1 teaspoon gin

½ teaspoon sugar

¼ teaspoon salt

1½ teaspoons kosher mock oyster sauce

½ teaspoon soy sauce

1 teaspoon cornstarch

pinch freshly ground white pepper

½ pound skinless, boneless chicken
breast, cut into ½-inch cubes

SAUCE:

2 teaspoons kosher mock oyster sauce
or vegetarian mushroom sauce

½ teaspoon sugar

1 teaspoon soy sauce

½ teaspoon Asian sesame oil

2 teaspoons cornstarch

pinch freshly ground white pepper

5 tablespoons chicken stock

3½ tablespoons vegetable oil

1 tablespoon minced fresh gingerroot

¼ teaspoon salt

¼ pound fresh mushrooms,
    cut into ¼-inch slices

¼ pound snow peas, strings
    removed, and cut on the
diagonal into 3-inch pieces

¼ cup bamboo shoots, cut
    into ½-inch pieces

4 water chestnuts, cut into
    ¼-inch slices

1 tablespoon minced garlic

1 tablespoon gin

1. Combine the marinade ingredients with the chicken and let sit for at least 30 minutes.
2. Combine the sauce ingredients and set aside.
3. Heat 2 tablespoons of oil in a wok over high heat until smoking and add the ginger and salt and stir-fry for 10 seconds.
4. Add the mushrooms, snow peas, bamboo shoots, water chestnuts and stir-fry for 2 minutes. Remove the mixture and set aside.
5. Wipe out the wok and reheat the remaining oil on high heat. Add the garlic and when it begins to brown, add the chicken with its marinade.
6. Stir-fry for 2 minutes.
7. Add the gin and stir-fry for another minute.
8. Add the reserved vegetables and stir-fry for 2 minutes. Add the sauce mixture and cook until it thickens.

BRAISED CHICKEN WITH GINGER   4–6 servings

This recipe is said to be good for stomach ailments and pregnant women.
Al Young, originally from Canton, served this dish to my wife when she felt
sick during the early months of her pregnancies.

> 1 frying chicken, cut, bones
>   and all, into 16 pieces
>
> MARINADE:
>   1 teaspoon kosher salt
>   1½ tablespoons sugar
>   5 tablespoons soy sauce
>   1 teaspoon Asian sesame oil
>
>   3 tablespoons vegetable oil
>   3 cloves garlic
>   6 slices fresh ginger, each
>   the size of a quarter
>   4 scallions, cut into 1-inch pieces
>   6 dried black mushrooms,
>   soaked and softened
>   1 tablespoon sherry

1. Mix the marinade ingredients and pour over the chicken.
   Let sit for as long as one day in the refrigerator.
2. Heat the oil in a wok and add the garlic, ginger and scallions
   and stir-fry for 1 minute.
3. Add the chicken and mushrooms and stir-fry for 2 minutes.
4. Add the sherry and stir. Cover wok and turn the heat to low.
5. Cook for 30 minutes until chicken is tender. Stir several
   times during cooking.

CHINESE ROAST CHICKEN

4–6 servings

In the Chinatowns of major cities, grocery store windows contain roast chickens hanging, golden and glistening. For a while, health authorities tried to prevent this "unsanitary" display, but the Chinese communities pointed out that roast chickens and ducks have been hung at room temperature for thousands of years without ill effects. They won.

MARINADE:

2 cloves garlic, minced

4 tablespoons soy sauce

3 thin slices fresh ginger

½ teaspoon five spice powder

1 teaspoon salt

1 teaspoon sugar

½ teaspoon pepper

1 chicken, 4–5 pounds

1. Mix all the marinade ingredients thoroughly.
2. Marinate the chicken for at least 3 hours and up to one day.
3. Preheat the oven to 350ºF and roast the chicken on a rack over a pan of water to catch the drippings until the chicken is golden brown, basting with the marinade at 15-minute intervals and turning the bird occasionally. Allow 30 minutes roasting time per pound.
4. Chop the bird, bones and all, with a cleaver and serve.

ROAST BARBEQUED TURKEY SERVED IN STEAMED YEAST BUNS

4–6 servings

Barbequed pork is a mainstay of many Chinese dishes and soups and I'm told it's delicious. Here is a kosher version which, when served in steamed raised buns, makes for excellent eating.

2 pounds turkey breast

MARINADE:

5 tablespoons soy sauce
2 tablespoons water
3 tablespoons brown sugar
1 tablespoon honey
1 teaspoon five spice powder
2 cloves garlic, minced
3 scallions, sliced

cilantro, for garnish
¼ cup hoisin sauce plus
  1 tablespoon water

1. Cut the turkey into pieces 5 inches long, 2 inches thick and 1–2 inches wide. This allows for greater absorption of the marinade.
2. Make the marinade and add the meat, turning it several times for 1½ hours.
3. Preheat the oven to 350ºF and roast the meat for 25–30 minutes on a rack over a pan of water to catch the drippings.
4. Cool and slice the turkey diagonally; garnish with cilantro, and place in steamed yeast bun (see following recipe) with a teaspoon of hoisin sauce and water mixture.

STEAMED YEAST BUNS

1. Take one recipe of bun dough or buy pizza or another bread dough.
2. Break into balls about 2 inches in diameter and roll out.
3. Smear the surface with Asian sesame oil and then fold one side back to make a half moon.
4. Let rise ½ hour and then steam for 10–15 minutes.

A HOSPITAL now stands at the location of Kaifeng's synogogue. However eight torahs from the synogogue are preserved in museums.

EGG FOO YUNG

4–6 servings

I remember from my youth a kind of omelet covered with a thick sauce at Chinese American restaurants. Authentic Egg Foo Yung does not have a goopy sauce. I like to serve it with the dumpling dipping sauce. This is a good recipe to use with cooked meats.

5 tablespoons vegetable oil
1 cup shredded cooked
   chicken or turkey
½ cup finely shredded
   scallions, white part only
½ cup bean sprouts
¼ cup shredded celery or
   chopped water chestnuts
¼ cup thinly sliced fresh mushrooms
¼ cup shredded napa cabbage
1 teaspoon kosher salt
⅛ teaspoon pepper
6 large eggs, well beaten

1. Heat 2 tablespoons of oil in a wok until hot. Add the meat and vegetables and stir-fry for 15 seconds.
2. Add the salt and pepper; stir-fry for 1 minute and remove the meat and vegetables.
3. Beat the eggs in a large bowl and add the meat-vegetable mixture.
4. Add the remaining oil to a wok and heat until very hot. Add the egg mixture in small batches and cook until the bottom is crusty. Flip over with a spatula and cook until just done, while the inside is still soft.

LEMON CHICKEN
4–6 servings

This is the ultimate lemon chicken, modified from a recipe published many years ago in the *New York Times*. Yes, it does use an entire 1-ounce bottle of lemon extract; but you won't believe how great this dish is.

4 boneless chicken breasts

MARINADE:
2 tablespoons soy sauce
1 teaspoon salt
¼ teaspoon Asian sesame oil
1 tablespoon gin or vodka

3 egg whites, beaten
1 cup water chestnut flour
  or cornstarch
¼ cup vegetable oil
¾ cup white sugar
½ cup white distilled vinegar
1 cup chicken stock
1 tablespoon cornstarch
2 tablespoons water
juice of one lemon
peel of one lemon, minced
1 1-ounce bottle lemon extract
3 small carrots, julienned
½ large green bell pepper, julienned
½ cup crushed pineapple
¼ head iceberg lettuce,
  coarsely chopped

1. Marinate the chicken breasts for 30 minutes.
2. Dip the breasts in egg whites and then in water chestnut flour.
3. Heat the oil until hot in a wok or pan and fry chicken breasts until golden.
4. Simmer the remaining ingredients, except for vegetables and lemon extract, in a pot until thickened.
5. Add the vegetables and pineapple and simmer for 15 seconds. Remove from the flame and add lemon extract.
6. Slice the chicken crosswise and place on the lettuce bed with sauce on top.

Chef's Hint: Water chestnut flour, found in Chinese markets, really makes this dish special. It is kosher by the standards used in this book.

ROAST DUCK IN A BAG   4–6 servings

Cooking a whole duck in a home kitchen creates a "fat bomb." There is almost no way to avoid duck grease all over the place. What follows is an attempt to make a reasonably authentic roast duck without the mess. It's the way I cook it when I do banquets.

> 1 duckling
> scallion

MARINADE:

> 2 tablespoons minced scallion
> 1 teaspoon white pepper
> 1 teaspoon salt
> 1 teaspoon minced garlic
> 1 teaspoon minced fresh ginger
> ½ teaspoon five spice powder

> 1 large potato
> 1 roasting bag, dusted with
>   flour on the inside
> 1 cucumber, peeled, seeded
>   and julienned
> several scallions, julienned
> ½ cup hoisin sauce mixed
>   with 2 tablespoons water
> Mu shu wrappers

GLAZE:

> 2 tablespoons sherry
> 3 tablespoons soy sauce

1. Remove the giblets from the duck interior. Combine and
   smear the marinade on the inside and outside of the duck
   and let sit for 15 minutes. Smear on the glaze.

2. Cut the potato crosswise into ½-inch slices. Arrange
   them on the bottom of the roasting bag and put the duck
   on top, breast side up. Tie the bag and make several small
   slits in it.

3. Roast at 450°F for 20 minutes, and lower the heat to
   350°F. Roast the duck for 40 minutes more. The duck
   fat will drain around the potato slices, which, by the
   way, will be poached in the fat. These potato slices are
   incredibly delicious, but very bad for your health. Try
   one anyway.

4. Remove the duck. Cut into pieces, bones and all, or
   thinly slice the breasts and place a piece on top of some
   cucumber, scallions and a teaspoon of hoisin sauce in a
   mu shu wrapper or tortilla; fold and eat.

TEA-SMOKED DUCK BREAST   2 servings

I think tea smoked duck breast is better than Peking duck. To make it, you need to get two duck breasts with skin. You can cut these from a whole duck and then roast out the rest for the meat in steamed buns or other dishes. If you are lucky, you can get breasts already cut from the duck.

MARINADE:

2 tablespoons minced scallion
1 teaspoon white pepper
3 teaspoons salt
1 teaspoon minced fresh ginger
½ teaspoon ground star anise

2 duck breasts
2 tablespoons Asian sesame oil
2 tablespoons black tea leaves
2 tablespoons brown sugar
1 teaspoon dried orange peel

1. Mix the marinade ingredients and marinate the duck breasts for 1 day.
2. Place the duck breasts on an oiled pan in a steamer and steam until tender, for about 30 minutes–1 hour, depending on the size of the breasts. Cool.
3. Brush Asian sesame oil on the duck.
4. Place the tea, sugar and orange peel on a piece of heavy-duty aluminum foil and seal the foil. Prick some holes in the top of the package to allow smoke to exit.
5. Place the foil package in the bottom of a wok and then put the steamed duck on a steamer pan above the foil package. Turn the wok onto high heat and cover tightly.
6. Smoke the duck for 1 hour. Turn off the heat under the

wok and let it completely cool to settle the smoke. The duck should turn a dark, smoky brown. Shred and serve as you would Peking Duck with Hoisin Sauce and Mandarin Pancakes.

Chef's Hint: To make the skin crispy, before steaming the duck, place the breasts skin-side down in a lightly oiled frying pan and sauté until crisp. You can also prepare turkey or chicken thighs the same way. Delicious! However, don't use chicken breasts or turkey breasts – they will dry out.

PAN ROASTED DUCK

4–6 servings

This recipe is modified from one published in the *New York Times*. The cooking method merges pan roasting in the French style with Chinese flavors to actually achieve the same end – delicious Chinese roast duck. It is my preferred way to cook duck.

1 duck, 4 to 5 pounds
1 teaspoon salt
½ teaspoon white pepper
2 tablespoons dry sherry
3 tablespoons soy sauce
2 tablespoons water
½ cup brown sugar
1 cinnamon stick, about 3 inches long
7 slices fresh ginger, about ¼-inch thick
4 pieces whole star anise
1 teaspoon coriander seeds
2 cloves

1. Cut the duck into 6 or 8 serving pieces; discard wing tips, back and neck.
2. Place the duck, skin-side down, in a heavy skillet over high heat and sprinkle with salt and pepper.
3. When the duck begins to sizzle, cover the skillet and turn the heat to medium.
4. After 15 minutes, turn duck over.
5. Cook for 15 more minutes; uncover skillet and raise the heat to medium high.
6. Cook until done, turning the duck so it browns on both sides for about 15 more minutes.

7. Remove the duck to a plate and pour off all but 1 tablespoon of fat. Leave any solids in the pan.
8. Add the sherry, soy sauce and 2 tablespoons of water and bring to a boil. Stir in remaining ingredients.
9. Once the mixture bubbles, return the duck to the pan and cook, turning it frequently, until sauce is thick and duck is well glazed, for about 5 to 10 minutes.
9. Remove the duck. Strain the sauce and spoon over the duck.

Chef's Hint: You can replace the ginger, coriander seeds and star anise with 1 tablespoon of Chinese Five Spice Powder. This prepared powder can be found in most supermarket spice racks or Chinese markets.

BEEF

Chinese beef dishes are excellent, and a good substitute for many pork dishes. Beef is not widely used in China, although lamb is found in the northern provinces. Nevertheless, Chinese cuisine has adapted beautifully to beef.

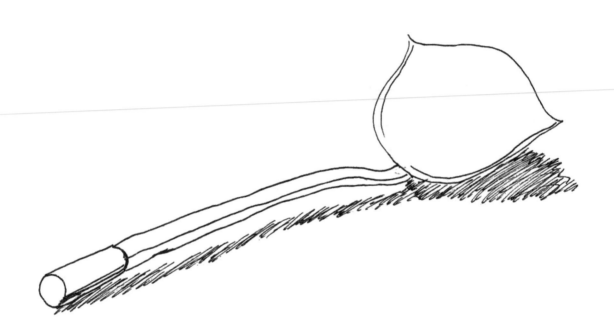

BEEF WITH GINGER AND GARLIC 4–6 servings

This is a simple and delicious dish served with rice.

MARINADE:
    2 cloves garlic
    1 tablespoon oil
    1 tablespoon lemon juice
    1 piece fresh ginger,
      1–1 ½ inches, minced
    1 tablespoon honey
    1 medium onion, sliced

    1 pound flank steak
    ¼ cup vegetable oil
    2 teaspoons cornstarch
    2 tablespoons soy sauce
    1 tablespoon sherry

1. Process all the marinade ingredients and pour over the meat.
2. Marinate overnight in the refrigerator.
3. Slice the meat across grain very thin. Dust with cornstarch. Stir-fry in oil for 3 minutes and remove to a serving dish.
4. Add soy sauce and sherry to the wok. Scrape up the dark bits remaining in the wok, dissolving them and pour over the meat.

BEEF WITH ONIONS

4–6 servings

This is also a very delicious and easy dish.

4 tablespoons oil
24 scallions, sliced into large pieces
4 thin slices fresh ginger
1 pound beef, thinly sliced
2 teaspoons cornstarch
2 teaspoons sugar
4 teaspoons sherry
4 teaspoons soy sauce
2 teaspoons salt
1 tablespoon cornstarch mixed
  with 2 tablespoons water

1. Stir-fry the scallions and ginger in 1 tablespoon of oil for 1 minute and set aside.
2. Dust the beef with cornstarch and stir-fry in the remaining oil until it loses its color.
3. Add the scallions and remaining ingredients and thicken with cornstarch and water to desired consistency.

BEEF WITH BROCCOLI   4–6 servings

This dish is an old standby of American-Chinese restaurants. Kids and people who are not keen on hot and spicy Chinese food like it.

½ pound beef
1 tablespoon cornstarch
2 tablespoons soy sauce
1 tablespoon sherry
2 tablespoons water
4 tablespoons vegetable oil
1 clove garlic, minced
2 slices fresh ginger, minced
1 teaspoon Asian sesame oil
1 pound broccoli florets
½ cup chicken stock
1 tablespoon cornstarch mixed
   with 2 tablespoons water
1 scallion, sliced into 1-inch
   diagonal pieces

1. Slice the beef thinly.
2. Blend the cornstarch, soy sauce, sherry and water.
3. Heat 2 tablespoons of vegetable oil in a wok and stir-fry garlic and ginger for 15 seconds and then add the beef and continue to cook until it loses its color. Set aside.
4. Add the Asian sesame oil and stir-fry the broccoli until coated and then add the stock, beef and cornstarch mixture and cover.
5. Cook for 1 minute and serve with the scallions.

BRAISED CURRIED BEEF AND POTATOES

4–6 servings

This is a remarkably delicious dish, a combination of near and far eastern cuisines.

2 tablespoons vegetable oil
1 pound beef chuck, cut
   into 1-inch pieces
½ teaspoon salt
4 white onions, sliced thin
4 tablespoons curry powder
1 tablespoon minced fresh ginger
1 tablespoon sherry
4 tablespoons water
1 teaspoon sugar
1 pound potatoes, peeled and
   cubed into 1-inch pieces
1½ cups chicken stock
1 tablespoon cornstarch mixed
   with 2 tablespoons water

1. Heat the oil in a wok and brown the beef, salt and onions together.
2. Add the curry powder and blend. Add the ginger, sherry, water and sugar and cook for 2 minutes.
3. Add the potatoes and stock and simmer for 30–40 minutes.
4. Thicken with cornstarch.

Chef's Hint: Sweet potatoes would be a good substitute for the white potatoes.

LAMB WITH LEEKS

4–6 servings

This recipe is so good that when I first made it, everyone ate so much of it they just about got sick. We couldn't stop.

MARINADE:

2 tablespoons soy sauce

2 tablespoons water

1½ tablespoons minced fresh ginger

1 tablespoon sherry

1 tablespoon cornstarch

1 teaspoon sugar

2 teaspoons cornstarch

1½ pounds lamb, cut into strips

5 tablespoons vegetable oil

2 leeks, shredded

SAUCE:

2 tablespoons soy sauce

2 tablespoons sherry

½ teaspoon sugar

1. Mix the marinade ingredients together. Add the lamb and marinate for at least 1 hour.
2. Stir-fry lamb in 4 tablespoons of hot oil until it loses its color. Add the sauce and stir-fry for another minute.
3. Remove the lamb and clean the wok. Stir-fry the leeks in 1 tablespoon of oil until they just get soft.
4. Add and toss with the lamb and serve with Mandarin pancakes with hoisin sauce, diluted with water, to make a medium thin sauce.

BEEF OR LAMB WITH SCALLIONS   4–6 servings

This recipe is almost as good as the previous one with lamb, and, given the cost, especially good for banquets.

MARINADE:

2 tablespoons soy sauce

2 tablespoons water

1 tablespoon sherry

1 tablespoon cornstarch

1 teaspoon sugar

2 teaspoons cornstarch

1 ½ pounds lamb or beef,
  cut into thin strips

6 tablespoons vegetable oil

4 cups shredded scallions (4 bunches)

SAUCE:

2 tablespoons soy sauce

2 tablespoons sherry

1 tablespoon Asian sesame oil

2 teaspoons Chinese or regular
  Worcestershire sauce

4 cloves garlic, sliced

1. Mix the marinade ingredients together. Add the meat and marinate for at least 1 hour. Stir-fry in 4 tablespoons of oil until the meat loses its color. Add the sauce, mix and remove from the wok.

2. Clean the wok, add 2 tablespoons of oil and then stir-fry the scallions until they wilt.

3. Add the cooked meat and mix with the wilted scallions. Serve with Mandarin pancakes spread with hoisin sauce diluted with water to make a medium thin sauce.

RED COOKED BEEF

Red cooked beef is a very, very good stew.

3 tablespoons vegetable oil
2-inch piece fresh ginger, thinly sliced
1 clove garlic, thinly sliced
1 pound beef, cut into 1-inch cubes
2 cups water
2 scallions, cut into 1-inch pieces
5 tablespoons soy sauce
1 teaspoon sugar
1 whole star anise
1 turnip, cut into large cubes

1. Heat the oil in a pot or wok and fry the ginger, garlic, scallions and beef for 5 minutes.
2. Cover with water and add soy sauce, sugar, star anise and cook, covered, until the beef is tender.
3. Add the turnip and simmer until the turnip is soft.

Chef's Hint: You can save the sauce and use it over and over, or use the sauce from a previously cooked red cooked chicken. It gets better and better. Freeze the sauce if you don't anticipate using it often.

SPICY SZECHWAN BEEF

MARINADE:

3 tablespoons soy sauce

1 tablespoon sherry

1 teaspoon sugar

½ teaspoon minced fresh ginger

1 pound flank steak, julienned very finely

⅓ cup vegetable oil

½ cup very finely shredded carrots

1 cup very finely shredded celery

¼ cup finely shredded hot green
   chili pepper or to taste

4 dried hot red chili peppers

2 teaspoons cornstarch

1 teaspoon Asian sesame oil

½ teaspoon ground Szechwan
   peppercorns or white pepper

1. Combine the marinade ingredients and marinate the meat for at least
   30 minutes.
2. Heat 2 tablespoons of oil in a wok until hot.
3. Stir-fry the carrots, celery and fresh chili pepper for 1 minute, then
   transfer to a serving platter.
4. Wipe out the wok. Add the remaining oil; heat the dried chili peppers
   (breaking them open) and lower the heat. Stir-fry until the peppers
   are dark brown. Dust beef with cornstarch and add.
5. Turn the heat to high and stir-fry for about 5 minutes, or until all
   liquid evaporates.
6. Add and mix meat with the cooked vegetables, Asian sesame oil and
   peppercorns.

点心

DESSERTS

Chinese dinners typically end with something simple, such as sliced oranges. Watermelon actually is ubiquitous as a dessert in many authentic Chinese dinners. Unlike Western cooking, there are few elaborate desserts. In my dinners, however, I have created and modified a number of desserts that have the spirit of Chinese cooking, but are also attractive to Western tastes and make a wonderful ending to a Chinese dinner. They might be considered some kind of "fusion" Chinese cooking.

ALMOND COOKIES

A standard Chinese cookie. this recipe appeared in *The Thousand Recipe Chinese Cookbook* by Gloria Miller.

> 35 almonds
> 10 almonds
> 1 cup sugar
> 1 cup white vegetable shortening
> 1 egg
> 1 teaspoon almond extract
> 2½ cups flour
> 1½ teaspoons baking powder

1. Blanch the almonds. Leave the first quantity whole.
2. Grind the remainder to a fine powder, with half the sugar, in a processor.
3. Preheat the oven to 350°F.
4. Cream together the shortening and the remaining sugar. Beat the egg and add, along with the ground almond mixture and almond extract.
5. Mix the dry ingredients together. Add to the creamed mixture.
6. Pinch off walnut-sized pieces of dough and roll into balls.
7. Grease the baking sheet. Arrange the cookies on the sheet. Press a whole almond in the middle of each cookie.
8. Bake in the middle of the oven for 15 minutes.

SWEET WALNUT OR PEANUT SOUP

The Chinese often serve sweet soups for dessert. This is a very nice one, modified from a recipe by Millie Chan.

> 2 cups shelled walnuts or peanuts
> ¼ cup rice flour (found
>   in Asian markets)
> 4 tablespoons of sugar
> 7 dates, chopped
> 4 cups water
> 1 teaspoon candied ginger
>   (found in Asian markets)

1. Place all the ingredients with 2 of cups water in a blender and mix until smooth.
2. Pour the blended mixture into a saucepan and bring to a boil. Simmer, stirring to prevent burning. Add the remaining 2 cups of water and serve warm.

SWEET BUNS WITH BEAN PASTE

Sweet red bean paste is a traditional stuffing for Chinese desserts. One famous such dessert is Eight Treasure Rice Pudding, which is far too complicated for my tastes, despite a wonderful flavor. Here is one way to use this paste to great effect.

THE BEAN PASTE:

½ pound dried adzuki red beans

4 cups water

¾ cup sugar or honey

¾ cup vegetable oil

THE DOUGH:

1 cup lukewarm water

1 package yeast

¼ cup sugar

1 tablespoon vegetable oil

1 teaspoon salt

2–3 cups flour

1. Rinse the beans. Pour the water in a pot. Add the beans and bring to a boil. Simmer for 1–2 hours until the beans are very soft and the water has been absorbed.
2. Combine with the sugar and oil.
3. Put the bean mixture in a lightly oiled frying pan and stir over very low heat for 5 minutes to slightly dry out and mash until smooth.
4. Make sweet yeast dough by mixing all the dough ingredients together, kneading until smooth. Place the dough in an oiled bowl; cover and let rise for 1 hour.
5. Punch down the dough and then make the buns, filling them with the bean paste, as described in the Dim Sum section of this book.
6. Steam or bake buns for a nice dessert.

ALMOND FLOAT

4–6 servings

This float is a delightful and refreshing end to a Chinese meal. I've modified it from a recipe in *The Thousand Recipe Chinese Cookbook* by Gloria Miller.

> 1½ envelopes gelatin
> ½ cup water
> 1 cup evaporated milk
> 3 cups water
> 4 tablespoons sugar
> 1 tablespoon almond extract
> 1 small can mandarin oranges,
>   lichee nuts or fruit cocktail
>
> 2–3 cups sweetened water
> (2 cups water + ½ cup sugar)

1. Add the gelatin to ½ cup of water to soften it.
2. Heat the milk and 3 cups of water. Pour in the sugar and stir until dissolved. Do not boil.
3. Add the gelatin and cook, constantly stirring the liquid until the gelatin is completely dissolved. Cool slightly and stir in the almond extract.
4. Pour the liquid into a shallow pan and refrigerate for at least one hour until the gelatin solidifies.
5. To make sweetened water, bring water to a boil. Stir in the sugar and cook, stirring, until dissolved. Let cool, then refrigerate until chilled.
6. Cut the almond gelatin into 3-inch diamonds and place in bowls with fruit.
7. Pour ¼ cup of sweetened water per person over the almond gelatin and serve.

CHINESE PANCAKES WITH APRICOT FILLING AND PEANUTS

This is an excellent dessert, a winner.

CRÈPE BATTER:

3 large eggs, well beaten

½ teaspoon salt

¼ teaspoon sugar

2 tablespoons melted butter or oil

1 cup water

¾ cup flour

1. Stir and mix all the ingredients until smooth. If foamy, let stand until the foam has subsided, for about 15–30 minutes.
2. Heat a 6-inch pan until a drop of water sizzles. Lower the heat to medium.
3. Brush the pan with melted butter or oil and continue to do so before each use.
4. Pour 2 tablespoons of batter into the pan.
5. Quickly turn and roll the pan until the batter is evenly distributed. Pour off any excess.
6. Brown until the edges appear dry. Turn out onto a dish towel. Do not stack. Stir batter often while making leaves.

FILLING:

2 pounds whole canned apricots

¼ cup water

3 tablespoons oil

2 tablespoons cornstarch

1. Drain the apricots and reserve ½ cup of liquid.

2. Cook the apricots in a pot with the liquid until they can be mashed down for about 3 minutes.
3. Add the oil and cook until the mixture forms a paste. Blend in the cornstarch to thicken.

TOPPING:

> 2 cups peanuts
>
> 1 cup sugar

1. Grind peanuts with the sugar, being careful not to make a paste.

ASSEMBLY:

1. Place 2 tablespoons of filling onto crèpe and roll as an egg roll.
2. Fry gently until light brown.
3. Place on a serving plate. Sprinkle 1 tablespoon of ground peanuts and sugar on top and serve.
4. If desired, melted semi-sweet chocolate can be drizzled on top.

BANANA AND GINGER WONTONS WITH CHOCOLATE SAUCE   8 servings

This is my favorite dessert. It first appeared in a column by Bev Bennett in a 1989 issue of the *Los Angeles Times*. Many natural foods stores sell candied gingerroot, already prepared. If you find it, you simply chop it up into ⅛-inch dice.

>   16 small wonton wrappers
>   1 banana
>   8 rounded teaspoons minced,
>   crystallized gingerroot
>   1 egg, beaten
>   oil

CHOCOLATE SAUCE:
>   2 ounces semisweet or
>   bittersweet chocolate
>   2 tablespoons butter or margarine
>   2 tablespoons brown sugar
>   ¼ cup whipping cream, non-dairy
>   creamer or orange juice
>   ¼ teaspoon vanilla (if using
>   whipping cream)

1. Cut the banana into chunks about ½–¾-inch thick.
2. Place one banana chunk on one side of each wonton skin.
3. Sprinkle 1 rounded teaspoon of crystallized gingerroot onto banana.
4. Brush edges of each wrapper with beaten egg and place another wrapper on top, pressing wrapper away from

banana to seal. Do not let too much air into area around banana.

5. Heat 2 inches of oil to 375ºF and fry wontons until golden on each side. Remove and drain them on a paper towel.

6. Serve with chocolate sauce on the side as a dip or pour over the wontons.

CHINA IS one of only a very few nations with no history of persecuting Jews because of their faith.

Crystallized Ginger

This is not a difficult recipe; but it needs to be watched, and the heat regulated carefully, so that all goes slowly.

> 1 cup peeled and minced fresh ginger
> 1⅓ cups sugar
> 1 cup water

1. Peel the outside brown skin off the root.
2. Mince the ginger, either in a food processor or with a knife.
3. Bring the sugar and water to a boil.
4. Add the minced ginger.
5. Simmer for 20 minutes until the syrup is greatly reduced.
6. Strain the ginger from the syrup and spread on the waxed paper.
7. When dry, sprinkle with the sugar and toss.
8. Store in a glass jar in a cool, dark place.

Chef's Hint: Do not discard the ginger syrup. It makes an incredible basting sauce for chicken or turkey.

BANANA-PECAN SPRING ROLLS WITH CARAMEL-RUM SAUCE

6 servings

This recipe is modified from a recipe in Bon Appétit, September 1997.

SAUCE:

    1 cup sugar
    ½ cup water
    ¾ cup whipping cream or
        nondairy creamer
    1½ tablespoons dark rum

1. Stir the sugar and a ½ cup of water in a heavy medium saucepan over medium-low heat until the sugar dissolves.
2. Increase the heat and boil until the syrup turns deep amber, brushing down the sides of the pan with a wet pastry brush and swirling the pan occasionally for about 12 minutes.
3. Reduce the heat to low. Add the cream (mixture will bubble vigorously) and stir until the caramel bits dissolve. Remove from heat.
4. Mix in the rum.

ROLLS:

    12 spring roll wrappers
    3 small bananas, peeled, quartered
        lengthwise, trimmed to 4 inches
    ¼ cup crystallized ginger
    ¼ cup finely chopped candied pecans
    vegetable oil (for deep-frying)
    powdered sugar
    Chinese five spice powder

1. Arrange 4 spring roll wrappers on the work surface (keep the remainder covered).

2. Place 1 banana piece diagonally across 1 corner of each wrapper. Brush the opposite corner with water.

3. Drizzle each banana with 1 teaspoon of caramel sauce, 1 teaspoon of crystallized ginger and 1 teaspoon candied pecans (see page 105).

4. Fold in the wrapper corner closest to the banana. Roll the wrapper over the banana once, then fold in the sides and roll up as for egg roll, pressing ends to seal. Repeat filling and rolling remaining wrappers. (Can be made 2 hours ahead. Cover and chill.)

5. Pour enough oil into a heavy large saucepan to reach a depth of 3 inches and heat the oil to 375ºF.

6. Fry the rolls in batches in the oil until a deep golden brown, turning frequently for about 3 minutes per batch.

7. Using a slotted spoon, transfer the rolls to paper towels and drain. Arrange 2 rolls on each plate. Sift the powdered sugar over them. Sprinkle with the five spice powder. Drizzle the caramel sauce around rolls and serve.

FIVE SPICE ROASTED PEARS
4 servings

Adapted from Gourmet Magazine, October 2001.

2 teaspoons unsalted butter or
margarine, cut into bits
4 firm-ripe Bosc pears, peeled,
halved lengthwise and cored
1 tablespoon fresh lemon juice
3 tablespoons water
1½ tablespoons sugar
¼ teaspoon five spice powder
2 teaspoons sesame seeds, toasted

1. Preheat oven to 375°F. Grease an 11 x 7-inch glass or ceramic baking dish with some butter.
2. Brush the pears all over with the lemon juice and put in baking dish, cut side down.
3. Pour water around the pears and scatter the remaining butter in the dish. Sprinkle the pears with the sugar and five spice powder.
4. Bake, uncovered, in the middle of the oven, brushing frequently with pan juices, until the pears are tender and golden brown, for 15 to 20 minutes.
5. While the pears are cooking, toast the sesame seeds in a dry pan. Watch carefully, as they burn easily.
6. Serve the pears warm, drizzled with some pan juices and sprinkled with the toasted sesame seeds.

DEEP-FRIED BANANAS WITH SYRUP AND TOASTED SESAME SEEDS

People can't get enough of these tasty morsels.

2 bananas sliced into ½-inch pieces

BATTER:
⅓ cup cornstarch
⅔ cup flour
water
oil for frying

SAUCE:
1 cup sugar
½ cup water
3 tablespoons sesame seeds

1. Slice the bananas into ½-inch thick pieces.
2. Mix the cornstarch and flour together with enough water to make a fairly thick batter, much like pancake batter.
3. Toss the banana pieces in the batter, and fry in very hot oil in batches until golden.
4. Combine the water and sugar and boil until you have a thin sweet syrup.
5. Put the sesame seeds onto a hot frying pan and toast until slightly brown and remove. Mix the bananas, syrup and seeds together and serve.

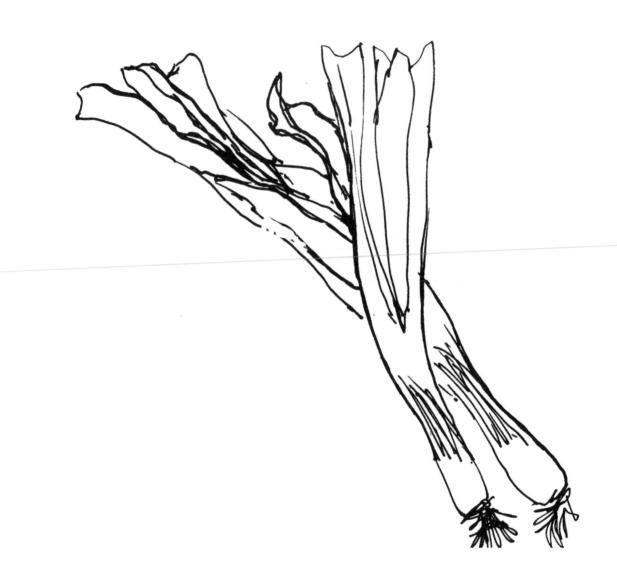

SELECTED REFERENCES

Asia Recipe, 2005 (http://asiarecipe.com/kosher.html)

Chang, M., 1990, *Kosher Chinese Cookbook*, Harmony Books, New York.

Chung, H., 1978, Henry Chung's *Hunan Style Chinese Cookbook*, Harmony Books, New York.

Goldstein, J. ed., 1999, *The Jews of China*, vol. 1 and vol. 2: *Historical and Comparative Perspectives*, Armonk: M.E. Sharpe, New York.

Tuchman, D. and Levine, H., 1992, "New York Jews and Chinese Food: The Social Construction of an Ethnic Pattern," *Contemporary Ethnography*. Vol. 22, pp. 382–407.

White, T., 1978, *In Search Of History: A Personal Recollection*, Harper & Row Publishers, New York.

Witchel, A., 2003, "For Some, It's a Very Moo Shu Christmas," December 17, *New York Times*.

INDEX OF INGREDIENTS AND GENERAL ITEMS

ALMOND
    Almond Cookies 195
    Almond Float........................ 198

APPETIZERS. *See* Dim Sum

APRICOT
    Chinese Pancakes with Apricot
       Filling and Peanuts .. 199–200

ASPARAGUS
    Stir Fried Fish Strips
    with Asparagus 142

BAKING SODA............... 41, 113

BANANA
    Banana and Ginger Wontons
       with Chocolate Sauce.. 201–2
    Banana-Pecan Spring Rolls with
       Caramel-Rum Sauce ... 204–5
    Deep-Fried Bananas with Syrup
       and Toasted Sesame Seeds ..207

BEAN CURD 28, 30

BEEF
    Beef or Lambs with
       Scallions....................... 188–9
    with Broccoli...........................185
    with Ginger and Garlic..........183
    with Onions 184
    Braised Curried Beef and
       Potatoes...........................186
    Red Cooked 190
    Spicy Szechwan 191

BEIJING................................15, 17

BETH SHOLOM
    CHEVRA SHAS............. 11, 13

BRAISED
    Chicken with Ginger 168
    Curried Beef and Potatoes....186
    Hot and Sour Fish............. 144–5

BROCCOLI
    Beef with 185
    Salad 125

BUNS
    Baked 88
    Barbequed Meat Buns 92
    Chicken-Filled Buns...............90
    Curry Buns 93
    Mushroom Cashew Buns........ 91
    Pan-Fried Pot Sticker Buns.....89
    Roast Barbequed Turkey
        served in Steamed
        Yeast Buns 170
    Steamed Yeast Buns 171
    Steamed Buns
        (The Traditional Way)........87
    Sweet Buns with
        Bean Paste 197

CABBAGE
    Hot Spicy Cabbage.................104
    Sweet and Sour Chinese
        Cabbage, Cold...................126

CANDIED
    Candied Pecan or Walnuts ...105
    Uncle Tai's Diced Chicken
        with Walnuts 162–3

CARAMEL
    Banana-Pecan
        Spring Rolls with
        Caramel-Rum Sauce ... 204–5
    Candied Pecan or Walnuts ...105
    Wings Karper............................ 61

CELLOPHANE
NOODLES......29, 72, 107, 109, 127
CHESTNUTS
    Water Chestnuts 14, 28, 75,
                        97, 109
    Rock Sugar-Ginger
        Chicken with Tofu
        and Chestnuts.............. 164–5

CHICKEN
    Braised.................................. 168
    Chinese Style Oven-Fried
        Chicken........................... 160
    Egg Foo Yung.........................172
    -Filled Buns 90
    General Tao's..................... 158–9
    Wings 60, 61, 62, 63
    Kung Pao 156–7
    Lemon Chicken 173–4
    Moo Goo Gai Pan 166–7
    Oven Fried 160
    Paper-Wrapped 99–100
    Red Cooked 154–5
    Roast 169
    Rock Sugar-Ginger
        Chicken with Tofu
        and Chestnuts.............. 164–5
    Steamed Chicken with Soy
        Scallions Sauce.................153
    Stock 47
    Uncle Tai's Diced Chicken
        with Walnuts 162–3

CHILI PEPPER
    Ants Climbing a Tree....109–110

Sweet and Sour Chinese
  Cabbage, Cold..................126
General Tso's Chicken 158–9
Kung Pao Chicken 156–7
Spicy Dumplings with
  Sesame Sauce 73
Spicy Szechwan Beef.............191

CHILI SAUCE 30

CHINA ROAD
  RESTAURANT 11, 14, 139

CHINATOWN 15, 21 39

CHINESE-AMERICAN
COOKING
  Chow Mein 14, 23, 115
  Corn Soup............................52
  Egg Rolls........................ 79–80
  Moo Goo Gai Pan 13, 166–7
  Sweet and Sour Fried Fish ... 148–9
  Wings Karper 61

CHOPPING AND SLICING ..32

CHOPSTICKS 17

CHOU EN-LAI......................27

CHOW DYNASTY 17

CHRISTMAS 22

CHUNG KING....................14

CINNAMON
  Pan Roasted Duck.................179
  Red Cooked Chicken.............154

CONFUCIUS 17, 18
COOKIES
  Almond Cookies 195

COOKING TECHNIQUES 31

CORIANDER
  Basic Dumpling Sauce.............70
  Chow Fun 113–4
  Chrysanthemum Hot Pot 54–5
  Fish Toast 102
  Meat and Noodle
    Spring Roll 82–3
  Pan Roasted Duck.................179
  Paper-Wrapped Chicken ..99–100
  Seafood Dumplings 75

CORNSTARCH....14, 34–5, 41, 43

CRYSTALLIZED GINGER
  Crystallized Ginger, Basic.....203
  Banana and Ginger Wontons
    with Chocolate Sauce ... 201–2
  Banana-Pecan Spring Rolls with
    Caramel-Rum Sauce ... 204–5

CURRY
  Braised Curried Beef
    and Potatoes....................186
  Buns..................................93

DAIKON RADISH
  Sweet and Sour Daikon
    Radish 103

DEEP-FAT FRYING

Chinese Style Oven-Fried
Chicken...........................160–1
Egg Rolls and
Spring Rolls.................. 79–83
General Tso's Chicken 158–9

DESSERTS

Almond Cookies 195
Almond Float......................... 198
Banana and Ginger
Wontons with
Chocolate Sauce 201–2
Banana-Pecan Spring Rolls with
Caramel-Rum Sauce ... 204–5
Chinese Pancakes with Apricot
Filling and Peanuts.. 199–200
Crystallized Ginger................203
Deep-Fried Bananas with
Syrup and Toasted
Sesame Seed.......................207
Five Spice Roasted Pears 206
Sweet Buns with
Bean Paste 197
Sweet Walnut or
Peanut Soup 196

DIM SUM

Assorted.......................... 95–105
Buns 85–93
Chicken Wings.................. 60–63
Dumplings 65–77
Spring Rolls and
Egg Rolls 79–83

DUCK

Pan Roasted Duck........... 179–80
Roast Duck in a Bag......... 175–6
Tea-Smoked
Duck Breast.................. 177–8

DUMPLINGS

Basic Dumpling Dough...........86
Basic Dumpling Sauce............70
Hunan-Style............................ 71
Seafood..................................75
Skins 66
Soup-Filled Juicy..................76–7
Soup Wontons 50–1
Spicy Dumpling with
Sesame Sauce 73–4
Vegetarian...............................72

EGG ROLLS 79

EGGS

Chinese Pancakes with Apricot
Filling and Peanuts...........199
Chrysanthemum Hot Pot .. 54–5
Egg Drop Soup 49
Egg Foo Yung........................172
Fried Rice 120–1
Tea Eggs 101

EGGPLANT

Szechwan Spicy Eggplant .. 129–30

FISH

Asian Fish in Packets 143
Braised Hot and
Sour Fish 144–5

Fish Toast 102
Salt and Pepper Fish Strips ... 141
Seafood Dumplings 75
Steamed Fish with Ginger
    and Scallions 139–40
Stir Fried Fish Strips with
    Asparagus 142
Sweet and Sour
    Fried Fish..................... 148–9
Red Cooked Whole Fish .. 146–7

FIVE SPICE POWDER
Five Spice Roasted Pears 206
Pan Roasted Duck.........179–180

GARLIC
Beef or Lamb with
    Scallions....................... 188–9
Beef with Ginger
    and Garlic..........................183
Double Cooked String
    Beans..................................136
Lo Mein with Peanut
    Sauce 111–2
Meat and Noodle Spring
    Roll 82–3
P.F. Chang's Lettuce
    Wraps 97–8
Peanut Wings...........................63
Soy Wings 62
Szechwan Noodles 118–9

GINGER
Banana and Ginger Wontons
    with Chocolate Sauce... 201–2

Beef with Ginger and
    Garlic 183
Braised Chicken with
    Ginger 168
Crystallized Ginger...............203
Rock Sugar-Ginger Chicken with
    Tofu and Chestnuts...... 164–5
Steamed Fish with Ginger
    and Scallions 139–40

GLUTEN
Ants Climbing a Tree....109–110
Hot Sour Soup 53

GREENS
Deep Fried Chinese Greens..135
Stir-Fried Spinach or
    Other Greens 131

HOISIN
Chicken-Filled Buns...............90
Chrysanthemum Hot Pot .. 54–5
Double Cooked String Beans..136
P.F. Chang's Lettuce
    Wraps 97–8
General Tso's Chicken 158–9
Roast Barbequed Turkey
    in Steamed Yeast Buns.... 170
Roast Duck in a Bag.......... 175–6
Tea Smoked Duck Breast.. 177–8

HOT AND SOUR
Braised Hot and Sour Fish.. 144–5

HUNAN
Hot Sour Soup 53
Hunan–Style Dumplings 71

Kung Pao Chicken 156–7

KAIFENG 19–20

KASHRUT LAWS 26

KOSHER .. 13–4, 23, 25–30, 39–43

LA CHOY 14

LAMB
  Beef or Lamb with
    Scallions 188–9
  Curry Buns 93
  Lamb with Leeks 187

LEEKS
  Lamb with Leeks 187

LEMON
  Lemon Chicken 173–4

LETTUCE
  Lettuce Wraps 97–8
  Lo Mein with Peanut Sauce .. 111–2

LOKSHEN 14

MANDARIN PANCAKES
  Mandarin Pancakes, Basic ... 128
  Tea–Smoked Duck
    Breast 177–8
  Vegetable Mu Shu 127

MARCO POLO 19

MARINATING 41

MEAT SUBSTITUTIONS 40

MING 19

MONGOLIA 17

MUSHROOM
  Black Mushroom,
    Dried 48, 127, 146, 168
  Banquet Soup 57
  Chow Mein 115–6
  Chrysanthemum Hot Pot .. 54–5
  Egg Foo Yung 172
  Moo Goo Gai Pan 166–7
  Mushroom Cashew Buns 91
  Tofu and Mushrooms
    in Vinegar Sauce 132
  Shiitake Mushroom 53, 55, 72,
    81, 90, 97, 99, 109, 132, 164

NOODLES
  Ants Climbing a Tree 109–110
  Chow Fun 113–4
  Chow Mein 115–6
  Lo Mein with Peanut Sauce.. 111–2
  Rice Noodles 54, 109, 113
  Szechwan Noodles 118–9
  Noodles in Brown Sauce 117
  Cellophane Noodles 72, 127

ONIONS
  Beef with 184
  Braised Curried Beef
    and Potatoes 186
  Curry Buns 93
  Onion Cakes 96

ORANGE PEEL
  Red Cooked Chicken 154–5
  Tea-Smoked Duck Breast 177–8

OYSTER SAUCE
Chow Fun 113–4
Szechwan Noodles............ 118–9
Moo Goo Gai Pan 166–7

PEANUT BUTTER
Lo Mein with
    Peanut Sauce 111–2
Szechwan Noodles............ 118–9
Peanut Wings............................63
Spicy Dumplings with
    Sesame Sauce 73–4

PEANUT
Peanut Butter 63, 73–4,
                                    111–2, 118–9
Chinese Pancakes with
    Apricot Filling and ..199–200
Kung Pao Chicken 156–7
Peanut Wings............................63
Sweet Peanut Soup.................196

PEARS
Five spice Roasted Pears........206

PEPPER
Red Pepper.....104, 109, 113, 156
Salt and Pepper Fish Strips ... 141
Chili Pepper... 126, 156, 158, 191

PORK 26–7, 40

POTATOES
Braised Curried Beef and
    Potatoes..............................186

RED COOKED
Beef 190

Chicken 154–5
Whole Fish 146–7

RICE
Rice Cooking 42
Rice Noodles......29, 54, 113, 115
Rice Sticks 29
Rice Wine....................28, 39–40
Fried Rice 120

RUM
Banana-Pecan Spring Rolls with
    Caramel–Rum Sauce .. 204–5

SAFE TREIF.......................21, 27

SANTOKU KNIFE..................32

SCALLION
A Basic Stir-Fry Dish 35
Beef or Lamb with
    Scallions...................... 188–9
Chrysanthemum Hot Pot .. 54–5
Lo Mein with
    Peanut Sauce 111–2
Soy Wings 62
Steamed Chicken with Soy
    Scallion Sauce 153
Steamed Fish with Ginger
    and Scallions 139–40

SESAME OIL...................... 30, 40

SESAME SEEDS
Deep-Fried Bananas with
    Syrup and Toasted
    Sesame Seeds 207

Spicy Dumplings with
 Sesame Sauce 73–4

SHANGHAI 19

SHERRY 14, 17, 28, 37, 39

SILK ROAD 19

SKINS 66

SOUP
 Banquet Soup 57
 Corn Soup 52
 Chrysanthemum Hot Pot .. 54–5
 Egg Drop Soup 49
 Hot Sour Soup 53
 Soup-Filled Juicy
  Dumplings 76–7
 Soup Wontons 50–1
 Sweet Peanut Soup 196
 West Lake Soup 56

SOY SAUCE 14, 23, 28

SPRING ROLLS
 Vegetarian 81, 204
 Meat and Noodle 82

STEAMING 16, 31, 36–7

STIR FRY DISH, BASIC 35

STIR FRYING 31, 33–6, 40–1

SUGAR
 Rock Sugar-Ginger Chicken with
  Tofu and Chestnuts 164–5
 Syrup 203, 204, 207

SZECHWAN
 Hot Sour Soup 53
 Spicy Szechwan Beef 191
 Szechwan Noodles 118–9
 Szechwan Peppercorn 16, 28,
        73, 191
 Szechwan Spicy Eggplant .. 129–30

TAOISM 18

TEA
 Tea Eggs 101
 Tea-Smoked Duck
  Breast 177–8

TOFU
 Chrysanthemum Hot Pot .. 54–5
 Hot Sour Soup 53
 Mapo Tofu 133–4
 Rock Sugar-Ginger
  Chicken with Tofu
  and Chestnuts 164–5
 Tofu and Mushrooms
  in Vinegar Sauce 132
 Vegetable Mu Shu 127
 Vegetarian Dumplings 72

VEAL
 Curry Buns 93
 Hunan-Style Dumplings 71
 Mapo Tofu 133
 Noodles in Brown Sauce 117
 Soup-Filled Juicy
  Dumplings 76
 Soup Wontons 50–1

Spicy Dumplings with
    Sesame Sauce 73
Vegetarian Spring Roll 81

VEGETABLE KNIFE 32

VINEGAR
Tofu and Mushrooms in
    Vinegar Sauce 132

WALNUT
Candied 105

Sweet Walnut Soup 196
Uncle Tai's Diced Chicken
    with Walnuts 162–3

WATER CHESTNUTS 75, 81,
    97, 102, 109, 164–5, 166–7, 172

WOK 33–4, 36–7, 69

WONTONS 50–1, 201–2

WRAPS 97–8

INDEX OF RECIPES

Almond Cookies 195

Almond Float........................ 198

Ants Climbing a Tree....109–110

Asian Fish in Packets 143

Baked Buns 88

Banana and Ginger
    Wontons with
      Chocolate Sauce 201

Banana-Pecan
    Spring Rolls with
      Caramel-Rum Sauce 204

Banquet Soup 57

Barbequed Meat Buns 92

Basic Dumpling Dough...........86

Basic Dumpling Sauce.............70

Beef or Lamb with
    Scallions........................... 188

Beef with Broccoli..................185

Beef with Ginger and Garlic.183

Beef with Onions 184

Braised Chicken with
    Ginger 168

Braised Curried Beef
    and Potatoes.....................186

Braised Hot and Sour Fish....144

Broccoli Salad 125

Candied Pecans or
    Walnuts 105

Chicken Stock........................... 47

Chicken Wings.........................60

Chicken-Filled buns 90

Chinese Pancakes with
    Apricot Filling and
      Peanuts..............................199

Chinese Style Oven-Fried
    Chicken............................ 160

Chow Fun 113–4

Chow Mein 115–6

Chrysanthemum Hot Pot 54

Corn Soup................................52

Crystallized Ginger................203
Curry Buns 93
Deep-Fried Bananas
     with Syrup and
     Toasted Sesame Seeds 207
Deep-Fried Chinese Greens....135
Double Cooked String Beans..136
Dumpling Skins
Egg Drop Soup 49
Egg Foo Yung.........................172
Fermented Black Beans.. 28, 133
Fish Toast 102
Five Spice Roasted Pears 206
Fried Rice 120
General Tso's Chicken 158
Hot Sour Soup 53
Hot Spicy Cabbage.................104
Hunan-Style Dumplings 71
Kung Pao Chicken 156
Lamb with Leeks 187
Lemon Chicken 173–4
Lo Mein with Peanut Sauce .. 111
Mandarin Pancakes 128
Mapo Tofu.............................133
Meat and Noodle
     Spring Roll 82–83
Moo Goo Gai Pan 166
Mushroom Cashew Buns........ 91
Noodles in Brown Sauce 117
Onion Cakes...........................96
P.F. Chang's Lettuce Wraps .. 97–8
Pan-Fried Pot Sticker Buns.....89
Pan Roasted Duck........... 179–80

Paper-Wrapped Chicken .. 99–100
Peanut Wings..........................63
Red Cooked Beef................... 190
Red Cooked Chicken.............154
Red Cooked Whole Fish 146
Roast Barbequed Turkey
     in Steamed Yeast Buns.... 170
Roast Chicken, Chinese 169
Roast Duck in a Bag.......... 175–6
Rock Sugar-Ginger Chicken
     with Tofu and Chestnuts...164
Salt and Pepper Fish Strips ... 141
Seafood Dumplings 75
Soup-Filled Juicy Dumplings....76
Soup Wontons 50
Soy Wings 62
Spicy Dumplings with
     Sesame Sauce 73–4
Spicy Szechwan Beef............. 191
Steamed Buns
     (The Traditional Way)........87
Steamed Yeast Buns 171
Steamed Chicken with
     Soy Scallions Sauce 153
Steamed Fish with Ginger
     and Scallions.....................139
Stir fry dish, basic 35
Stir-Fried Fish Strips
     with Asparagus 142
Stir-Fried Spinach and
     Other Greens 131
Sweet and Sour Chinese
     Cabbage, Cold...................126

Sweet and Sour
    Daikon Radish 103
Sweet and Sour Fried Fish ... 148
Sweet Buns with
    Bean Paste 197
Sweet Walnut or
    Peanut Soup 196
Szechwan Noodles 118–9
Szechwan
    Peppercorn 16, 28, 73, 191
Szechwan Spicy Eggplant......129
Tea Eggs 101

Tea-Smoked Duck Breast . 177–8
Tofu and Mushrooms
    in Vinegar Sauce..............132
Uncle Tai's Diced
    Chicken with Walnuts 162
Vegetable Mu Shu 127
Vegetable Stock 48
Vegetarian Dumplings 72
Vegetarian Spring Roll 81
West Lake Soup 56
Wings Karper............................ 61

IT'S GOOD TO EAT